# TO KNOW A STRANGER

# TO KNOW A STRANGER

ISABEL SENIOR

NEW DEGREE PRESS

TO KNOW A STRANGER

ISBN

978-1-63676-699-7   *Paperback*
978-1-63730-471-6   *Kindle Ebook*
978-1-63730-472-3   *Digital Ebook*

*To my mom, Diane, without whom I would not*
*have acquired a love of creative writing.*

*To my dad, David, and to Audrey, Jonathan, Nella, and many others,*
*for supporting and tolerating me throughout this writing process.*

*To the strangers who inspired this book and the strangers*
*who will continue to inspire me and others to be creative*
*and be our truest and best selves in the world.*

# CONTENTS

———

# AUTHOR'S NOTE

———

I am amazed by the generosity strangers have shown me at various points in my life, not in terms of tangible offerings but in the form of stories, beliefs, and experiences. And in turn, I feel grateful for the vulnerability they invoked in me, pushing me out of my comfort zone and into experiences that I never would have known. Like writing this book.

It has been particularly enjoyable to write this story now, as it has been a year of social isolation due to the pandemic with little opportunity to meet strangers and interact with the world outside my small community of friends and family.

That being said, I have to admit I am not much of a conversation starter. I worry people do not want to talk to me or selfishly that time spent with a stranger might not prove to be as valuable as time spent on any number of other activities. But I think the world needs conversation starters, and I aspire to offer my time and my ears next time someone gives me the opportunity, a small repayment for the impact strangers have had on me. I now know we all can be the "kind stranger" in someone else's story.

In many ways, the creation of Piper represents a compilation of people I have learned from, whether to be more like them or to better understand the thought processes and life experiences of people so different from myself.

I don't precisely remember the Romanian woman I met in Montreal six years ago who initially inspired Piper's character because I have written and re-written her so many times. But what I do remember is that she sat down with me and was willing to share thoughts and experiences I would think are too personal even to share with a best friend. Her openness inspired my interest in strangers and their stories.

A year later, while working in Beirut, Lebanon, another stranger lent hours to me. Many of the lessons Violet learns throughout this book are inspired by insights I received in that little bookstore coffee shop in Hamra. At the end of our conversation, she shared with me that she was not the kind of person who opened up easily but that something about me prompted her to share much deeper thoughts than she otherwise would have.

I tried to understand what it was she saw in me that made her want to open up. At the time, I was journaling regularly and wrote, *I think she saw a lot in me that she thought resembled her. But I think we may just both have anxiety.* I wonder if it is human nature to search in others what we see in ourselves? While the expression goes, "The eyes are the window of the soul," I have begun to wonder if others are actually the window to our soul. How we view strangers may reveal more about the way we view ourselves.

Violet's interaction with Piper not only gives her insights into a stranger's mind, but it also has a profound impact on the way she views the world and herself in it. While Violet shied away from embracing her own life, meeting Piper pushes her out of her protective shell, giving her the strength to accept others for who they are and, more importantly, to accept herself.

While I did not intend on writing myself into this book, it was only natural that many of my own insecurities and challenges integrated themselves into Violet's and Piper's characters. Rooting for them and searching for ways to enable them to overcome fears pushed my personal growth in ways I had not imagined possible.

## CHAPTER 1

# MONTREAL, QUEBEC, JUST FOR LAUGHS COMEDY FESTIVAL

———

"Excuse me!" I found myself pleading with two women in bright orange volunteer shirts. "Do you know where the volunteer van is?" I strained my ears in their direction, but noises flooded my mind. Boisterous laughs, screaming children, languages I didn't recognize, all flowing in the same direction: In. My instincts told me to evacuate, to make my way to the sidelines, to crawl under a table, but I stayed put.

Temporary metal barricades snaked through the blocks of the city where the festival took place, forcing festival-goers to form long lines. I had walked in circles around the perimeter countless times now only to see many versions of the same scene. Each line seemed to be longer than the next. I had no idea what would happen if I were to arrive late for my volunteering shift. And my phone was dying.

I breathed deeply, and the smell of sweat and fried food filled my nostrils. With a slow exhale, I let the uneven cobblestones ground me. I arched my feet as if to hug the stones tightly with my toes, a motion that by no means would prevent me from getting swept away or trampled by tourists, but it calmed me all the same.

Giving up on finding the volunteer entrance, I queued behind a family that couldn't quite keep track of their children, who made a game of passing in and out of the improvised barrier walls. Above me, a grand archway covered in cut-out HA HA HAs mocked me. The head of Victor, the green monster mascot of the comedy festival, was mounted atop the banner, warning me to turn back now or else.

From my spot in line, I called again to the two women who were just inside the festival perimeters, but they were unable to hear me or chose not to. After a final unanswered and awkward wave, I hugged my arms against my body, becoming a smaller version of myself as the people in front and behind me closed in on my bubble. Part of me wished I were sandwiched between my parents, who until recently were my usual escorts in these sorts of situations. At seventeen, I was expected more and more to be on my own to figure things out. I tried again to catch the volunteers' glances, unable to make sense of their expressions.

The women did not take their eyes off the line of tourists snaking through the metal barriers and entering under the archway. I noticed how they each clenched counters, clicking as menacingly as one could to mark the entrance of each tourist. In their place, I would have quickly lost focus. Even now my eyes curiously fixated first on the texting tween with the Chanel purse and then on the hulking man with a mohawk in front of me in line.

I finally made it to the front of the line and passed under the banner. *No attacks from Victor yet.* I chuckled to ease my nerves and tried again with the volunteers. One was young, maybe even my age, and discretely smoked a cigarette, which she held low in her non-clicker-clad hand. I waited until they counted me and asked again, "Do you know where the volunteer van is?"

The younger woman blew smoke in my face, which I wanted to swat away but didn't, nonetheless frustrated that she might have increased my chances of getting lung cancer or, more likely, that my mom would accuse me of smoking. She looked toward her older associate, who continued to stare over my shoulder at the incoming crowds, apparently committed to counting the exact number of festival-goers.

Turning in a circle, I hoped I would catch sight of a sign when the older woman glanced at me and then darted her gaze down an alleyway, as she gave a quick nod. I checked the pocket of my leggings for my phone before speed-walking in the direction she had indicated. "*Merci*," I shouted over my shoulder, finally loosened from clutches of the entrance line mob, but the women had turned back to their ceaseless task, and I doubted that she had heard me.

I wondered if they were mother and daughter or was their unfriendly demeanor a Quebecois thing? Why would they be so curt with a stranger? The French were stereotyped for their rudeness, but they weren't French, were they? Then it crossed my mind that they might not speak English. Maybe they didn't even speak the same language as each other. I considered the possibility of being assigned a shift with someone like them. The silence might have been nice.

Halfway down the alleyway, a guy in an orange staff shirt greeted me in unintelligible French. Was he trying to give me directions? I pulled out my phone to check how desperate I should be. 6:05 p.m.

"Do *you* know where the volunteer van is? Or, uh, wherever volunteers are supposed to go?" I asked.

He stroked the scruff on his chin, in what he, a fellow teenager, seemed to think was a wise-looking thing to do. While I knew it was uncool to be late, I thought it was a lot less cool to stroke a patchy beard, then pause to pull up low-hanging cargo pants.

"*Uh bénévoles? Ou? Bénévoles?*" I shuddered at my poor French but stammering the word *volunteer* seemed to be my best shot.

He perked up and pointed down the alleyway to the right, into what, from where we were standing, looked like a rundown construction site.

I offered a nod and a "*merci*," turning my speedwalk into a jog. Behind me, I could hear him shout, "*Attends! Pourquoi est-ce que t'es si pressée ma belle!*" Despite his thick Quebecois accent, I understood the catcall. I shuddered, wishing I could redirect his eyes from my butt.

Sure enough, the volunteer location doubled as a construction site. The landscape appeared to have once housed structures, which had been torn down, leaving behind three temporary trailers. Had there not been a scattering of people in matching neon t-shirts walking away from the trailers in small groups, I would have never imagined that I was in the right place.

I sighed and trudged along, trying to stay on the muddy plywood path. When I arrived at the first trailer, I paused to read a small cardboard sign on the door with two words scratched across its surface in black sharpie—*Bénévoles / Volunteers*.

*Finally.* I walked slowly up the steps and eased open the door. Inside, the room was already occupied by six adults, each sitting expectantly on a metal fold-up chair. I scanned the room for an empty chair, preferably a lone chair. With no luck, I tucked myself against the wall next to the entrance.

Overhearing conversations here and there, I picked up that the room was full of volunteers who had not yet been given a position but were there simply as backups in case someone else did not show up or reinforcements were needed. I imagined how, if the signs directing volunteers had been a bit clearer, the need for extras would have been eliminated. There wasn't anyone to check me in, and I realized this purgatory may have been my punishment for showing up late.

Miscellaneous pieces of paper hung arbitrarily, advertising lesser-known comedians who would be performing at the festival. I doubted any of them would become as famous as Jerry Seinfeld, who my mom said was a returning performer at Juste Pour Rire. I knew who Seinfeld was but the reference was a bit dated and didn't convince me that the festival was as cool as she had hoped.

A weekend's worth of mud caked the floor. My white Veja leather and suede sneakers suddenly seemed silly. I bought the shoes right before coming to Montreal, in an attempt to build my wardrobe into a euro chic, or I guess, Canada chic, collection rather than the athleisure of an American high schooler.

The man sitting closest to me looked about forty-five years old, and while I thought he appeared fatherly at first glance, I quickly noticed his missing teeth and the rat's tail that hung out from under his baseball cap. He leaned forward, watching three women who were sitting close together. Their volunteer shirts clung to their bulging bodies, and they laughed loudly. I tried to understand what they were saying to each other, but again the Quebequois French sounded like meaningless blabber. One would have thought the six years of French I had taken in school would get me somewhere, but even after having been in Montreal two weeks already, I had not adapted to the accent or vocabulary.

I tried to pick up anything. A word or a sentence I could understand and maybe use later, when and if I were to take up writing again. One of the women made direct eye contact with me, and I turned away. All my years of people watching and I still had not perfected the blank, "I'm not looking at you, just lost in thought," expression.

I felt again for my phone, and once reassured it was still in the side pocket, I clasped my hands together. Moisture collected on my palms and I released them, wiping them on my thighs. Maybe if I stood there unmoving in the entrance, the staff would choose me to fill the next position. Or better yet, they would send me home because they had enough faux volunteers, though I imagined my parents wouldn't appreciate that. This was *their* idea of what was good for *me*.

The door swung open, and I was almost run over by three young-looking volunteers: two guys, who looked no older than I was, and a slim young woman who was maybe in her twenties. With her dainty gold jewelry and the way she had cropped her volunteer shirt, she almost looked fashionable. I eyed her bare stomach and became self-conscious of the awkward way any cropped t-shirt felt on me. My body didn't curve inward at the waist, so the only thing crop tops did for me was show off my long and rectangular midsection.

The guys announced French-sounding names, and there was shuffling in the room. The volunteers who had been called followed their guides out the door.

"Violet Bell?" The woman's voice rang, and my hand shot up. Why would I raise my hand? She wasn't taking attendance.

"*Oui, c'est moi,*" I tried to redeem myself, quickly lowering my hand. I gave her a smile, hoping she would take pity on me and assign me somewhere good, or at least somewhere I wouldn't have to speak French. Options darted through my mind as my peppy guide motioned for me to stay put, which I did. She flitted out of the trailer.

When we found out we were coming to Montreal for the summer, my mom started planning my itinerary. After I declined full-day language school, volunteering at the Juste Pour Rire Comedy Festival seemed the next best option to my mom. My parents had no intention of volunteering themselves. My mom only signed me up, since apparently I was the one lacking in life experience. It was all decided weeks ahead of time without an enthusiastic endorsement from me.

On my second day in Montreal, I attended an info session with my parents on volunteering at the festival. Thankfully, the info session was hosted in English.

The beer-bellied sixty-something man in a fire-red track suit told us, "Make sure you smile, and be helpful whenever possible."

Great. The only useful information I managed to gather was my personal ranking of the best and worst positions I could be assigned. Best: Giving out programs at a stand-up comedy event. Worst: bussing tables. Using a clicker to count tourists, directing crowds, and serving aperitifs to VIPs fell somewhere in the middle.

My guide returned with a t-shirt, which she tossed to me with a smile.

I had barely pulled the XL getup over my head when she was shoving a piece of plastic attached to a lanyard into my hands and was out the door again, eyes glued to her clipboard. The t-shirt hung loosely around my torso. I placed the lanyard around my neck and glared at her petite frame from behind, wondering if the size t-shirt she picked was just by chance or if she was making a judgment about me.

A few hundred feet beyond the volunteer site and up a flight of cement stairs, she stopped and smiled even more broadly this time. *"Bienvenue à Juste Pour Rire!"* she said to me with her hands extended out. "Welcome to the Just for Laughs Comedy Festival!"

I too stopped and saw that from our vantage point, we could miraculously take in the festival in its entirety.

It was hard to make out the perimeter of the festival and how much of the city had been taken over by the annual event. From our point of view, the entirety of Montreal could have been a flood of tourists, food trucks, and outdoor amphitheaters, all branded with the image of Victor, the fuzzy green monster. I hadn't spent much time in cities, but from what I saw of Montreal before the festival began, I liked it more than New York City or Boston. When there weren't thousands of people rushing from performances to pop-up outdoor restaurants, Montreal felt manageable. I looked forward to when Montreal would be back to its usual self, unencumbered by all this festivity and raucous exuberance.

## CHAPTER 2

# MY ASSIGNMENT

---

Just as quickly as my grinning guide had stopped to admire the venue, she was on the move again. We weaved through even more tightly packed crowds, her swinging black ponytail my North Star. The buildings around us were modern, and streetlamps lit with colored bulbs lined the sidewalk, even though the differentiation between sidewalk and street was irrelevant. The area was closed off to cars, and people were everywhere. Ornately sculpted fountains lit up red, an odd choice for a flowing liquid, and the building facades shined in a faint, eerie glow, as if someone put a flashlight under their chin. Other than some of the star performers, who were in enormous auditoriums, nearly everything and everyone else remained outside.

Crowds formed open circles in the streets, and I knew that if we made our way through the ring of tourists, who were themselves balancing on their tiptoes, we would find dancers, magicians, and other street performers. We passed a raised gazebo that housed a colorfully painted acrobat distorting her body as a crowd oohed and ahhed. Street vendors wheeled carts of plush Victors and green foam fingers, trying to capture the attention of little children and their parents.

As we passed an open pavilion, I could see a man standing on a raised platform. The sun shone so brightly on him; it was hard to believe it was evening. He gestured to an enormous white cannon beside him, etched with black and red flames, and conveniently directed the crowd's eyes away from the forty-foot net that would inevitably catch him.

Despite never having attended the festival, I knew the act he would perform. On previous evenings, I had heard the cannon man's voice bellowing distantly from my family's temporary apartment a few blocks away.

"Ladiez and Gentlemen! I am 'ere today to preform za most daring, za most frightening, za most spectacular of act! But eet is up to *you* if you want me to do zis. I am too scared to do zis on my own. I need your encouragement!" His voice boomed as he pronounced each letter very carefully—*an-kou-ra-je-man.*

Like clockwork, thirty minutes past the hour each weekend evening, I could count on the same crowd-riling speech. My guide paused so we could witness the performer's plunge, but as he approached the cannon, I shifted my focus to the crowd. Everyone stood in a massive oval, encompassing the cannon man's set. A sea of heads tilted up, eyes wild in anticipation.

My guide and I stood for a moment on the periphery, her eyes strained toward the performance while mine were on a young father next to us who beamed at the spectacle, though I suspected his joy came not from the staged act but from the little girl with braided hair propped up on his shoulders and the little boy whose hand he grasped. He couldn't have seen but may have imagined how his daughter's dark brown eyes flickered in awe at the cannon man. The boy appeared to pull his dad's arm as he squeezed his eyes shut.

In less than a moment, the act was over and the performer leaped out of the landing net, bowing and speedily extending his hat to his viewers. The dad lowered his daughter and offered a few dollars to each of his kids, gesturing for them to make their way forward and tip the performer, who was expeditiously making his way through the crowd. But the little boy just shook his head. To my surprise, his sister offered him a hug, took the money their father offered, and whispered the consoling words, "It's okay. The man won't go boom again." Her brother looked her in the eyes, held his hand out for a dollar, and they bound off to thank the eager cannon man together.

I found myself smiling, and before my guide ran off again, I pulled out my phone and typed, *It's okay. The man won't go boom again*, in my notes app. I knew the man would go boom again, but it was believing he wouldn't that made the boy strong. My guide turned abruptly, and I quickly shot a picture of the cannon man before following her again. The photo would do nothing but sit in my camera roll. I had not written much in months; nevertheless, taking the photo was still instinctive.

Once we passed the pavilion, we were on an open street lined with food trucks. We navigated past overflowing lines and giddy tourists. An opening at the end of the line of food trucks revealed another crowd, circling a man atop a ten-foot-high unicycle. His striped shirt, rosy cheeks and curled mustache made me wonder if he was mimicking a mime, the French, or a French mime. After circling around a couple times with his arms flailing in a twitchy dance, he stopped and turned toward the audience.

"Now, I cannot finish my act without a brave volunteah." He drew out his "a"s into an "awe" sound and dropped the final "r" in "volunteer," like I had heard people do in Boston. He scanned the crowd, probably looking for an audience member who wouldn't get him killed. We were making our way past the act when his request came. I looked down and sped up until I could hear him shout, "You," in a different direction.

What would have happened if he had called on me? Would I have shouted back that I was in a rush? Or panic and pretend to faint? Or simply act as though I could not understand a single word he said? A crop of auburn hair moved toward the center of the circle, but before I could see if this brave volunteer would succeed in not harming the performer, we were already turning off of the main street and down an alley.

I had not realized how accustomed I had grown to the noise until it began to quiet. I sensed we were approaching another perimeter of the festival, and I crossed my fingers, hoping I wouldn't have to work at a check-in gate. But to my surprise, when we got to the end of the side street, it was a dead end, blocked off by enormous buildings. This was clearly not a tourist entrance to the festival. Ten-story buildings loomed above me, and I slowed my gait but my guide continued walking toward the doors of the building at the end of the alleyway. Had I gotten some sort of administrative job?

As we entered, my guide propped open the doors to the outside and stopped in the foyer, a ten-by-ten-foot room with a cement indoor-outdoor feel. The second set of doors that led into the building remained shut and there was no clear indication of what was behind them. Two metal folding chairs leaned up against the wall, and my guide grabbed one, set it up, and stood expectantly. The moment my butt hit the chair, she launched into an explanation of my evening, of which I understood half. Her French was quick with many Quebecois words replacing the continental French vocabulary I had learned in school.

I gathered that the building served as changing rooms and costume closets for some of the street performers at the festival. To prevent homeless people or lost tourists from entering the building, my job was to sit in this metal chair and ensure only people in crazy costumes passed through.

Before I could ask any questions like, "What if there is a vibrantly dressed homeless person?" Or add any comments like, "It feels a little problematic to be so anti-homelessness," my guide smiled and assured me that she would be back at 11:00 p.m. to relieve me from my shift and give me a raffle ticket for the chance to win a meet-and-greet with one of the famous Canadian comedians I had never heard of.

As my guide disappeared around the corner, I pulled out my phone. I leaned back and stretched my legs as scents from the food trucks wafted toward me. Instinctively, I opened my notes app again. But staring at the words I had written, I felt discomfort. It was the kind of feeling when you know you have something to do but even starting it provokes anxiety so you put it off. If you don't start, it can't go poorly. At least that is what I had been telling myself these days.

I opened Instagram and scrolled through smiling shots of my classmates at the beach, a group photo captioned *Dream Fifteen* with beer cans barely blurred out of the background, and Shelby and three girls from our grade at The Melting Pot. I knew I should close the app, but instead, I clicked on my own profile. I hadn't posted in nearly four months; my last photo was from junior prom, smiling with Shelby, our dates photobombing with goofy faces. 255 likes. I clicked on Shelby's tag and scrolled down to a photo from the same evening. It was a photo I had taken; she looked over her shoulder, her then-dyed-silver updo and bony back the focus of the photo. 468 likes.

*Low Battery* popped up and forced me out of my neon-screen-induced trance. Four and a half hours was a long time to stretch 20 percent battery, especially when I needed 5 percent at a minimum to map my way home. At least the cannon man's performance would signal the passing of time.

For the first time, I looked more closely at my lanyard. The cloth around my neck was bright orange and would have blended in with my shirt if it hadn't been for the pattern. Where there weren't "Ha"s written in white font, there were outlines of sharp white teeth that belonged to the recognizable Victor icon. Some sets of teeth were grinning, others were opened wide in an expression of shock. My least favorite were sticking out their snake-like tongues.

The badge itself was turquoise and green. It read *Juste Pour Rire. Just for Laughs. 2019* across the top and *Violet Bell. Bénévole* along the bottom. In between was a picture my dad had submitted for me. I knew it was my dad because my mom knew better than to submit a photo of me from when I had braces. My teeth had been metal-free for over a year now, but I assumed this image of me, slick ponytail and braces, was the first one he found, and seeing no problem with it, submitted it.

Even though I cringed at the photo, my face had matured only slightly in the last year. The photo was printed in a circle that the cartoon Victor clutched, mouth wide, as if my face was an appetizing treat.

I studied his face, trying to figure out why the people of Montreal had chosen to plaster his image all over the city. His green sharp nose matched his red horns in shape and size. Eyes wide and mouth open, his large teeth took up most of his face.

Letting the lanyard drop back into my lap, I closed my eyes and practiced breathing. In. Out. The knots in my stomach slowly began to loosen, but a day of anticipation had not done my body any favors. This wasn't too bad. This evening had sounded like a lot, especially since I had talked to almost no one but my parents for the past two weeks. And even then, it was mostly me and my mom finding brief touristy outings or me sitting on our couch plugged into Netflix and "writing college essays."

I appreciated the quiet, blissfully ignorant of what the night had in store for me. I continued to breathe, eyes shut, mind racing with the faces and voices of all the people I had passed in the street.

My heart rate slowed as I drifted into a daydream, so I nearly jumped out of my chair at the sound of a loud, "*Salut!*"

# CHAPTER 3

# MAKING A FRIEND

---

"*Je t'ai trouvé une amie!*" my smiling guide announced triumphantly.

I stared at her as she balanced energetically on the balls of her feet. She had disappeared only to reappear suddenly a quarter-hour later with another volunteer. I quickly wiped the sleepiness from my eyes, hoping she hadn't noticed my lack of passion for my work, albeit volunteer work.

"I found you a friend!" she repeated this time in perfect English.

I had understood the French but needed a little more explaining, which maybe she would do, now that I knew she spoke English.

Instead, she motioned for my new friend to move forward. I eyed the woman's imperfect though not yellow teeth as she gave a sideways glance to our guide. She had an obvious disinterest in formal introductions. As she stood there in silence, I inhaled deeply, anticipating the scent of recently smoked cigarettes or something but smelled nothing.

The guide's eyes showed me a twinge of pity as she attempted to nurture a connection between us. "*Elle s'appelle Daria,*" she said, introducing Daria.

Daria still said nothing.

The guide stood in silence for a moment longer, her smile becoming more and more forced as the seconds ticked by. She was saved by a crackling noise that came from the walkie-talkie strapped to her waist, and she turned away, bouncing out of the entryway and down the alleyway with a wave over her shoulder.

Once the guide was out of sight, Daria lurched past me to grab the second metal folding chair, which was positioned against the wall. I jerked forward, as if to show I would have gotten the chair for her had I thought of it. As she carried it over to where I was sitting, she let the metal legs drag against the floor, and I could feel the hairs on my arms rise. With a loud clang, she set up the chair about two feet to my left, also facing the doors that led out into the alley.

The knots were back. I tried to ignore the nauseous feeling between my ribs. I knew I was better off introducing myself right away, so at least we wouldn't have to do so after two hours when one of us needed to leave and find a bathroom or get some food. Despite this, I sat in continued silence, my mind focused on everything that could go wrong, every reason this woman would hate me, never wondering even for an instant if I would like her.

I wanted at least to get her name right, and by that point, I had already worried so much about what I would say that I forgot her name. I turned slightly so I could see her badge, but she leaned forward with her elbows on her knees, blocking my view of her nametag. Waiting for her to adjust herself in her chair, I looked straight ahead, focusing on faint sounds I could hear from the festival. People cheering at acts I tried to picture but couldn't, vendors calling out inflated prices for food and souvenirs.

Finally, the woman next to me sat up straighter to stretch her arms above her head, and I caught a glimpse of her name. *Daria Bucer.*

Before I could initiate an introduction, she turned to face me, and seeming to get over whatever irritation she felt when she arrived, she offered a smile.

I smiled back, turning my body to face her. "*Elle a dit que vous vous appelez Daria?*" I asked

She rolled her eyes. "Ah, you're an American. Just speak to me in English." I couldn't quite place her accent. I had only just now traveled outside of the United States and didn't want to assume any accent I might have heard on TV was correct. My best guess was Russian, but I knew better than to ask. Then again, she *had* targeted my accent.

"As for what to call me, please don't call me Daria again. That hyper organizer insisted on calling me my *official* name, but I go by Piper." She was so matter-of-fact with each word, smacking her lips at each "p."

"Nice to meet you, Piper." I repeated her name back to her, ingraining it in my memory so I wouldn't have to ask her again. "My name's Violet, and yeah, I'm American. I guess I have to work on my accent." I forced a giggle in an attempt to be likable, but it came out as more of a snort.

We were seated next to each other and had both turned back to face the open doors. Hardly anyone walked past the entrance, and those who did carried set pieces or sported headsets and held clipboards. The tall buildings cast shadows on the cracked cement ground of the alleyway.

I caught glances of Piper's face out of the corner of my eye. She had a Tiffani Theissen look about her, though to say she looked like the young hot Tiffani Theissen my mom fan-girled over from *Saved by the Bell* would have been a compliment.

She looked younger than my parents but not by that much. Her chin protruded from her heart-shaped face in almost a cute way, but then a smaller chin would appear when she leaned back to look down and check her phone. Skin was visible through her ripped jeans, and her too-large volunteer shirt hung down nearly to her thighs. Though probably the same size, my t-shirt went just past the top of my leggings. She didn't try to make the t-shirt look fashionable, like our beaming guide had. And yet her eyebrows were meticulously plucked and trimmed, and her winged eyeliner elongated her wide blue eyes. I couldn't decide if her dark silky ponytail was intentionally slicked back, or if it was simply the greasiness of unwashed hair.

I wished my mom had helped me apply eyeliner before leaving the apartment. I had begun wearing makeup when my acne flared up in ninth grade. I quickly learned it was not an art I was skilled in, and more time was spent trying to cover up what I saw as problematic rather than painting on something beautiful.

Piper's phone dinged from between her thighs, and she revealed an older model iPhone. The screen was cracked, but only along the edges, not hampering visibility. As she texted the person back, metal bangles clanged like a knife scratching a ceramic plate. It wasn't until she had sent the text, and then read the short response she got back, that she turned her head to face me again. This was going to be a long night.

"So, Violet, if you're an American, why the hell are you working here?" she asked.

Her abrasiveness was off-putting, so I chose my words carefully. "My dad's got a medical conference here, so my mom and I came with him to visit Quebec."

This was only partly true. He was in charge of running the medical conference, which was why we were staying in Montreal for most of my summer vacation but that wasn't information I needed to share with Piper if I wanted her to like me.

I could have stayed at home in Connecticut with my grandparents or gone to away camp like my brother. But instead, my parents decided it was best for me to be "pushed out of my comfort zone." My mom was an adolescent psychologist at a high school, which is how she got the summer off and why she forced me to come with her. When I protested, reminding her I would get out on my own when I left for college, she teased me, repeating, "Violet, you know Canada is one of the weakest forms of exposure therapy there is."

Piper hardly seemed to care about my answer, and while I thought about what to say, she blurted out, "No! Why *here*? Like why are you volunteering here?"

At the time, I didn't know there was a right answer. I accepted that it did seem odd an American teenager would choose to spend her Friday evening nobly protecting street performers from homeless people. "My parents made me sign up. They, um, really like to force me to do things I don't want to do."

She sighed and moved on. "Yeah, what is up with our job? What do they expect us to do if 'unauthorized personnel' show up?" She used her index and middle fingers to air quote the words "unauthorized personnel" and sneered as she mimicked our guide's attempt at politeness when she tried to explain our roles.

The worst thing I had imagined this job would entail was trying to come up with four and a half hours of conversation, but this brought on a new level of anxiety. What would in fact happen if someone unauthorized really did try to get into the building? "You have a good point there." My voice drifted off as if to continue, but there wasn't much else to say.

Feeling like I had to keep speaking, I asked the only question that popped into my head. "How did you choose the name Piper? It doesn't sound much like Daria." I immediately cringed at the judgmental tone of my words. I had heard of people moving to the States and changing their names because Americans couldn't pronounce their real name. What if this was one of those situations and I too had pronounced her name wrong, proving I was part of the problem, and then insisting that she explain it to me?

Instead, she gave a straightforward response. "Piper means pepper in Romanian, which I guess I like." I listened again to the way she pronounced Piper, wanting to get it right. Pee-pear. The "i" turned into an "e" sound, and the "r" at the end almost sounded French. It did explain why I couldn't place the accent. I had never met anyone from Romania, or any country similar to it. I knew it was in Europe but wouldn't have been able to place it on a map. Piper took my silence as a nudge for more information, like she hadn't fully answered the question. She huffed, "I don't know, I just felt like changing my name."

Perhaps it was as simple as that. I nodded as if I understood. I couldn't have imagined a more unrelatable explanation. My mind drifted to people who got tattoos just because they thought they were pretty. And even those people only existed in TV and movies. I had never met someone with a tattoo. A name change felt like a permanent decision that should be based on more than having a fondness for a common spice. There must have been more to the story that she wasn't telling me. I had let the silence drag on, so instead of following up on my nod, I turned to face straight forward down the alleyway, attempting to match her indifference.

# CHAPTER 4

# VIOLET'S BLOG

---

My wrist tickled, and I lifted my hand to swat off whatever had landed on me, but when I looked down, it was just a bead of sweat. Despite the fact that it was probably already 7:00, the sun shone bright in the sky and the air felt thick with moisture. I flexed my fingers, attempting to be discreet as I wiped my hands on my thighs again. I allowed myself to focus on my own body for another moment before freeing my mind to think about something else.

The scene of the young dad and his kids filled my brain, and I could feel myself speculating on how I might craft their lives in writing. I tried to push these thoughts down. The escapism I so often occupied myself with had in the last few months started making me feel uncomfortable. I let my eyes wander over to Piper, who seemed drawn away by thoughts of her own.

I kept thinking about how the little girl's words felt familiar to me. I had always been the reassuring sister to my little brother, while desperately masking the plethora of fearfulness that constituted my reality. But in the past few years, my brother had grown out of hand holding and pep talks, instead approaching crowds and chaos face-on at football games and bonfire parties. So I had taken on others to comfort, and when they couldn't be helped, I created characters in my mind who could be.

Well before I wrote stories, I told them, making up scenes in elementary school for my friends to perform on an imaginary stage under an oak tree in the schoolyard. Sometimes my friends were lost at sea, their only hope a massive stingray they had to befriend for directions to shore, or they were collegiate fencers battling it out for a national championship. But more often, my friends were normal people, afraid of their first day of school or fighting with their annoying brother. I never wrote our stories down. That thought never crossed my mind. It was just a game.

As my friends grew older, I found myself recounting stories in my head or to friends who wouldn't listen anymore because they had moved on from my charades. When it came time for middle school, I had forgotten about this entertainment entirely. That was, until my seventh grade English teacher assigned a "Day in my life" story for homework, due at the end of the week. I had always done well in English, managing good grades with few problems with my work. This was the first time we were asked to write a "story" in the place of an essay.

Wanting to impress my teacher, I thought about the assignment constantly. I carried my black and white composition notebook around with me, gathering what I thought were the most interesting elements of my day. I pieced each story together and proudly handed my composition in to my English teacher. When she handed it back to me, I saw that I had received a B+. She explained in the little blurb at the bottom of the page that, while the writing was quite good, I had not responded to the prompt.

I read through my "Day in my life" vignettes, and next to each of them in purple ink, she wrote, *This story isn't about you.* And at the end she wrote, *I want to see a day in* your *life.* As my face flushed, I regretted checking my grade while still in class, eyeing my peers who likely wrote about their last soccer game or dress rehearsal. No one else seemed to be agonizing over their grade. I wanted to protest my grade with my teacher, but I was not the kind of student who debated that sort of thing. Instead, I made sure to respond more directly to each prompt she gave me for the rest of the year, securing my A in the class.

Instead of dropping the matter, I continued to carry around my notebook, its black binding becoming loose as I filled it with the stories of people around me.

In the beginning, I wrote about what I saw. I wrote about people like our math teacher, Mrs. Goshen, whom I renamed Ms. Harrison. I would watch her at her lunch table as she measured out exactly one tablespoon of raisins, and then sprinkled them into her plain nonfat yogurt. She would chew loudly, even though there really was nothing chewable in the mixture. The other teachers didn't sit with her at lunch, so as the year went on, she began taking activities with her to the lunchroom. It began with math tests to grade, which turned into crossword puzzles and sudoku, until eventually she was bringing books with covers I would have thought too embarrassing to put on display in the lunchroom. Books about vampires and wizards, all filled with romance.

As my notebook's pages started to fray and the cover became splotchy with food stains and doodle marks, my stories wandered outside the grips of reality.

In my notebook, Ms. Harrison became a single mother of two children, whose development she worried about constantly. Listening to the other teachers' complaints about their students upset her, until she began sitting at her own lunch table. In this time of loneliness, she turned to fantasy novels, her form of escapism. When she finally decided to turn her life around, she picked up an evening class, which she hoped would propel her career so that she too could *graduate* from our dreadful middle school and move on to some fancy high school.

I had no evidence that any of this was true, but as I sat miserable in math class, I imagined she was in solidarity with me. And one day we would both be able to escape the horror that was Maplewood Middle School.

For my fifteenth birthday, my dad got me AirPods that I was careful not to lose. My brother didn't get me anything because we didn't get each other gifts, and my mom got me a beautiful new notebook. She didn't know what I wrote in my black and white one, but whenever she saw it on the kitchen counter or tucked into the front pocket of my backpack, she would ask why I didn't replace it. She'd even offered me a twenty dollar bill to go to Paper Source and pick out a new one. I always responded that it wasn't full yet. So she waited, ever perceptive, until she could see me working on the final pages before getting me a beautiful gold notebook with a real spine, not a weak paper one that constantly threatened to lose pages of my stories. The gold notebook came with a fine-point ink pen, but I continued to use my pencil, afraid to make mistakes in my new piece of art.

The only person whose persistence was strong enough to unfasten the metaphorical lock I kept on my notebooks was Shelby. I had initially kept my arm wrapped around the notebook as we loitered in classrooms after school before I had my license and could get us home. With time, I began covering up the pages less, inviting Shelby's ever-curious eyes to devour one paragraph at a time.

Eventually, Shelby was ignoring both her math homework and her phone to read the left side of my gold notebook while I scribbled across the right. It was unspoken between us that she read my writing. The few times Shelby did mention slivers of what I wrote, pointing out a high school administrator or lacrosse player who had cameoed in a short story, she was met with elbows blocking words and smudging graphite. While she took comfort in divulging intimate details of her life to me verbally and in the texts that she sent me when we weren't together, this became my version of opening up within our friendship. I appreciated that she never made me explain; she just read my stories and let me be.

One day, in the spring of ninth grade, I was up in my bedroom doing history homework after school when I received a text from Shelby.

*Read this and thought of you :) I loved it; you should check it out.* She followed the text with a link to a website I hadn't heard of.

I watched the "..." appear and disappear again, a contemplative follow-up. Finally, another text came through.

*I'm just going to put it out there, I could see someone sending the same text about one of your stories.* The "..." popped up one more time but vanished just as quickly.

I stared at her text for a moment, and then clicked on the link. It brought me to a blog post called "The Guilt From Saying How I Really Feel" by writer, thewaytomyheart. The whole piece took me no more than ten minutes to read, but I found myself reading it over and over. The first time absorbing the text. The second picturing Shelby, in the plant-filled oasis she built in her attic, skimming through the prose and reckoning she was beginning to understand me. The third trying to picture this author, who I presumed was a girl, maybe a little older than me. I imagined her writing this blog in her bed with tears in her eyes or in a public coffee shop, the world around her unaware of the narrative she was bringing to life. Each word represented raw emotion, digestible and human, a cry to share thoughts and feel a little less alone. The insecurity that seeped into her blog through imagery was strikingly unmerited. The fourth time I read the piece, I saw the stories from my gold notebook formatted beautifully on a blog page that was mine to share.

For months after, when I closed my eyes at night, I pictured the names and stories of my characters stretching across a computer screen. But in my dreams the screen wasn't mine. It belonged to a teenager who would never meet me and yet would come to know me through my writing.

There was no sudden moment, no sign that it was the right time, but on my sixteenth birthday, after I'd blown out my candles, played Scrabble with my family, and everyone had gone to bed, I gifted myself a four-dollar website domain. I had been scouring the internet, accumulating a mental list of blogs I loved, even leaving comments and engaging with usernames I recognized.

I found myself uploading a new story almost every week, each piece paired with an image that represented the protagonist of the story. I became motivated to finish all my homework and studying during the free periods at school that I didn't share with Shelby. Then, throughout the day, I'd sneak glances at my phone in my locker, a bathroom stall, even under my desk in class, checking to see what people thought of my stories. There were no assignments, no grades, no feedback on my grammar or thesis. Fellow authors pondered, asked questions, and even shared their own stories inspired by mine. I'd stay up at night responding to this world of people who cared about the people's stories I dissected online.

Over the following months, I also began to meet more people in my town, more people than I had met in the previous sixteen years of living there put together. Of course, I wasn't really meeting them. I had always been an observer, but now I was observing the people around me with a purpose. I watched, speculated, and then built lives for the people around me, and not just at school. Their names, locations, and even appearance changed, keeping them anonymous, but the inner turmoil I suspected they experienced filled out an invented reality that I imagined to be true. The single identifier that could have given them away was the pictures I took on my phone, but even those were not attributable to a single person. I never wrote about people I truly knew, whose stories were clear, displayed in front of me at my breakfast table or through late-night text messages. No, I preferred to imagine how other people's facial expressions and faltering words painted an abstract picture for me to make clear.

I was fully absorbed in this duality, my physical and digital worlds, filled with characters I had seen in person and brought to life online. I was exhilarated by the debates and friendships my stories fostered among my readers. I began to recognize usernames as they returned to like or comment on my stories, so in turn, I would stop by their pages to read their writing.

One username, neonhoops, returned often. I never brought it up with her, but I suspected this online fan was Shelby. How she found my blog would forever remain a mystery, and however she found me, I was glad. After all, she was my first loyal follower.

By my seventeenth birthday, I had nearly a thousand readers and dozens of, well, I wasn't sure they were friends, but we were connected by the words on our computer screens, bearing witness to each other's isolated minds.

When my mom tried to talk to me about why I didn't have more friends, especially once Shelby disappeared from my afterschool study sessions junior year, I didn't tell her about this internet community. She was of the generation that believed in "stranger danger" and would probably make me delete my website or at least make it private. Even worse, she would ask to read my writing.

But my website had been abandoned for almost three months now. The thought of writing brought a burning to my throat. Thoughts about Shelby, about my life, about what on earth I was doing living in some fantasy world made up in my head and playing itself out in my blog, even if the fantasies were about ordinary people at school or in cafes. I glanced sideways at Piper again, wondering if she had noticed the tenseness I could never seem to hide, according to my mom. But she was busy picking at her nails thinking about something I could only imagine.

# CHAPTER 5

# IF IT ISN'T FUN,
# MAKE IT FUNNY

———

After a few minutes of unmoving silence, interspersed by bangles clanging as Piper fidgeted in her chair, I blurted out, "So, what do you do?"

Piper looked up at me slightly askance. "My boyfriend," she quipped and laughed at her own joke before adding, "Um, I collect Nikes. I do stand-up." She elongated the words "Nikeeees" and "staaand uuup." She bobbed her head to one side and then the other, as if she were listing average hobbies. "Let's see. What else?"

I chuckled awkwardly, assuming she was joking around but not wanting to laugh too loudly in case she wasn't. Then the thought crossed my mind that she was unemployed and I had asked an incredibly insensitive question. I must have made a face because she rolled her eyes.

"I knew what you meant, but why the hell do you care about my job?" she laughed.

I didn't tell her that it was just a question I thought I was supposed to ask. A question that, if she were like any other adult I had met, would have launched her into a passionate, or at least instructional, monologue. In my defense, I uttered the spiel that usually earned me praise or respect from adults I'd meet through my parents, suggesting I was ambitious enough to already be focused on my own career and was trying to learn as much as I could before I had to choose a major in college.

She scoffed, and I immediately regretted my response. I knew how I looked in her eyes, and while I so desperately wanted to escape the privilege that oozed out of my pores, I wasn't sure I was being truthful with myself. It was more likely that I didn't want to be judged, and my fists re-curled, my nails digging into palms of baby skin. Piper's face was void of any condemnation, but I pictured her thoughts.

Despite not wanting to answer my question, Piper revealed she was an elementary school teacher. I felt my eyebrows raise and immediately lowered them, hoping she didn't catch my surprise. The swearing, sex joke, and overall spiciness would not exactly be my recipe for someone who works with children.

My hometown didn't produce teachers, but it wasn't that everyone had fancy jobs either. Some were stay-at-home moms. Most of the adults were businesspeople, lawyers, or doctors. There were some who had retired from these careers or whose kids had graduated from college and moved on, so they ran yoga studios or bake shops—their "dream jobs." There was just something about teaching that was under glorified. Maybe it was that most people paid others to deal with their kids. Why would they want a job where they were forced to do it themselves?

The nice thing about Piper being a teacher was, as a high schooler, I at least knew what that meant. I asked her what age she taught.

Piper described teaching her group of eight-year-olds as being pecked to death by twenty-five snot-covered chickens whose parents were roosters. I thought about my seven-year-old cousin, who insisted on screaming about people's butts and refused to do his homework. My aunt hired a full-time nanny even though she didn't have a job.

I felt anxiety for Piper, even though she seemed to have no fear about her job at all. Little kids never seemed to like me. It wasn't that they disliked me, but I didn't carry the big energy that would cause children to pick me out of a group and decide I was cool. Instead, being with children reminded me of the game I played in my head when I saw older girls. *Which girl would I like to be like when I grew up?* In the presence of young women, I'd stand up a little straighter and wonder what it would be like to be admired.

None of Piper's complaints about her job, beyond the mention of snot, actually had to do with the children. Instead, the administration brought a heat to her tone that I had not noticed before. And other teachers made her laugh, though not in a friendly way.

"You don't know how bad it is," she said, shaking her head. "We have to maintain 'the school's code of honor,'" she sneered, enjoying the freedom to mock the school administration. "Students can't congregate in the hallway. Students have to carry a bathroom slip if, God forbid, they have to pee. Students even have to sit in the same order, next to the same people every day." As she rattled off the rules, I thought it didn't sound so different from the elementary school I had attended, which was actually run pretty efficiently. But Piper practically spat at the notion that she should enforce these rules.

The rules didn't stop with the students. There were strictly dictated curricula and methods expected to be used by the teachers. And, to make matters worse, the teachers were evaluated quarterly by "superiors," teachers who had been working at the school longer.

"Get this," she said, turning to face me more directly, the back of her chair at her side, showing she meant business. "On my first day, I had to sit in on another teacher's classroom to get a sense of how things were run. Now, this teacher was praised by the school. Even won some rigged award the year before. So I show up, and the teacher put math problems on the board and asked kids to come up and solve them." She waved her hands to express her frustration at what she witnessed.

I mirrored an expression of shock, but let her continue, assuming something much worse would come.

"The kids did not talk to each other except at recess. And worse, none of the teachers participated in recess with their kids or wanted to have any fun at all, for that matter." She paused before saying thoughtfully, "I honestly wanted to save each and every child right then and there from the rigidity that is a one-way ticket to lackluster adulthood."

While I knew that she wasn't joking about it, everything she listed sounded pretty standard. I tried to imagine anything different, but my creativity fell short. "What's your classroom like? Like a typical day?"

"Typical?" Piper asked skeptically, laughing aloud once again. "There is no typical! Every day is a surprise."

Piper spent time in the evenings and over the summer reading articles and watching YouTube videos about engaging children, how to make them interested and not wipe away their individuality. Instead of memorizing vocabulary and writing math problems on the board, her kids wrote and performed their own plays about multiplication. Parents always reported that their kids were talking about math at home. When the other teachers weren't looking, her kids gathered and practiced their performances in the hallways. And on big performance days, everyone dressed up, with items supplied by Piper so as not to embarrass students who couldn't afford to buy new costumes. She also supplied snacks and little trinkets that made a clapping noise for after each performance.

Like the students, Piper's favorite part of the school day was recess. So they always had recess twice a day, while the other kids only had it once after lunch. However, the rule was that during their morning recess, they each had to do something creative. Then, during afternoon recess, they had to present what they had created that morning. Piper also participated in these presentations, often recounting wild, perhaps somewhat inappropriate stories to her class, energized by their rowdy responses.

Her eyes glinted as she spoke about working with her students. "For the most part, I get away with it. None of the parents complain because their kids are learning to read and do basic math just as quickly as the kids in the other classrooms. Kids are amazing. Whenever we have, or I have, quarterly reviews, all I have to do is prep my students. I always give them a third recess if we get a good score."

I imagined Piper as a real-life Ned Schneebly, except not doing anything illegal. I wasn't sure I would have liked having her as a teacher, though maybe I would have turned out differently if I had.

It struck me how Piper named each of her students as she spoke about them. Anne wasn't the troublemaker in her class two years ago who overfed the class fish; she was Anne. Braden wasn't the kid from Piper's first year teaching who spent his recess jittery with tears in his eyes; he was Braden. These kids, who to me didn't seem old enough to have true personalities and were only in Piper's class for a brief moment in time, were people contributing to Piper's life. And she was clearly a heroine in theirs.

I wished the parents of her students could see the shine in her eye as she spoke about their children.

I asked Piper if she had always wanted to be a teacher and was surprised by her ambivalence. "It was something I fell into," she answered, as if that explained it all.

"Huh," was all I could reply, hoping the silence would prompt her to continue.

And it did, of course. "If I had stayed in Romania, who knows what I'd be doing. Definitely not teaching!" She laughed. "Not unless they start paying teachers a hell of a lot better. No, it was my opportunity to travel, to leave home and try something new."

Even as she spoke, it was hard to believe her words. That she had been so haphazard about her job, seeing it as a means to try something new. And even now it seemed like she didn't take any of it seriously, more like a means to have fun, laugh, and joke around.

Everyone I met counseled me to find my dream job though no one asked me about my dreams.

"What? You don't like my answer?" Piper scoffed, and I realized I was still just gazing at her as lightbulbs were going on in my head.

"No, that all makes sense. I guess usually people make plans." I adjusted my gaze to her shoulder, muttering, "Or they study to become something."

I thought about what my parents would say if I decided I wanted to be a teacher. They would probably be supportive but unsure of why I wanted to throw away my potential. Then again, they had both endured eight years of medical school and additional training, so maybe they'd just be jealous I would be blessed with a shorter indoctrination into adulthood.

Piper's eyes wandered too. "Plans are stupid." She spoke definitively, eyes locked on the cement wall behind me. "They never go how they're meant to, so what's the point?"

I nodded but disagreed. They at least gave some direction, and I just avoided thinking about if it were the wrong one.

Piper wasn't done. "Look, I'll give you an example. If my boyfriend, Adrian, had had a plan, he'd be doing some boring-ass job. He'd been studying IT or something like that back in Romania. Oof. But he followed opportunity, not a plan, so now he gets to be the happiest person in the world."

I didn't feel like I knew that many happy people, so I didn't argue. As she spoke, her smile widened, and her voice softened. Adrian loved playing basketball and practiced constantly. One day, a scout came to one of his games, and next thing he knew, he was playing professionally in Romania, then moved on to France, and was eventually scouted by a US team in the NBA.

All I could think of was how jealous my brother would be that I met this woman, though I felt too awkward to ask her for her boyfriend's name.

"Don't look too impressed yet," she quipped. "He lasted an embarrassingly short amount of time in the States. Between injuries, quarrels with coaches, and many D-league games, he decided to try his luck in Canada. Not only were the people nicer, go figure, that move was the best he could have made."

She concluded by saying, "Adrian never would have planned to have the life he has. He wouldn't have even been able to dream it. I mean, no one could dream up the opportunity to date me." She was joking, but I could tell she was trying to get me to draw a conclusion. I didn't think like her. The idea that one day I'd grow up and date or move to a new city frightened me. So little of it felt in my control. Piper seemed to think that was a good thing, that it left room to chase opportunities, but for me, it made sense to stay grounded in the reality that was planned out for me.

Piper kept eye contact with me, waiting for an insight as though I were her student.

"Life's about adventures and, um, meeting people to share it with?" I practically whispered, hoping this was the takeaway point.

She seemed satisfied and nodded emphatically.

I wondered what life would be like if I were Piper. In some ways, it sounded freeing to believe things would work out. Though to let this happen would mean disregarding my plan, even if it wasn't entirely mine in the first place.

At my K-8 school, there was a "career fair," an event only open to eighth graders to prepare them for high school and life beyond. And when it came time to decide which career booths I'd visit, I had no idea. The dream world of youth had not yet let me move on to more adult ideas.

The gymnasium was set up in clusters. I eyed the doctors in lab coats, engineers in jeans, and bankers in suits on one side, and then the jumble of people who had undoubtedly studied humanities: a lawyer, an HR specialist, and a journalist. I wasn't necessarily drawn to any of the career titles displayed on their nametags, but I was certainly repelled by anything STEM.

The people staffing the booths were parents of students from my school. I didn't know what HR was, but the man at the booth was Alyssa's father, a girl who had bullied one of my best friends in sixth grade, so I opted for journalism instead. After listening to an older woman discuss the highs and lows of corporate journalism, I politely thanked her and moved on to the law booth. I didn't recognize the woman at the booth, so I reached out and shook her hand. She introduced herself as Ms. Pingly, a name unique enough that I felt comfortable asking if she was married to Mr. Pingly, my English teacher. She smiled and said she was, asking if I was a student of his. I quickly informed her that English was my favorite subject and that maybe I would study it in college.

Her eyes lit up as she launched into stories from when she studied English at the University of Connecticut. I listened, asked her a couple questions, and made room when other students approached the booth, knowing that the conversation was still just between me and Ms. Pingly. I left the career fair with a smile on my face, certain in that moment that I would major in English, even if it meant I had to become a lawyer. Had that been it, had I walked out of the gymnasium with one more reason to like Mr. Pingly and a small degree of interest in law, everything would have been great. But unfortunately, I had to go home and answer my parents' questions about how it went.

From then on, I was the little lawyer of the family. My parents, who were both in medical fields, knew nothing about the field of law. They researched different kinds of law, the LSAT and at what age I should take it, deciding on twenty-two, and learning everything there was to know about which universities had the best pre-law programs. Even though it earned a conspiring glance between my parents, I insisted on an English major being a part of the plan.

I was thirteen years old, and suddenly my extended family members began asking me about my interest in law. Their wide smiles only slackened slightly when I admitted how little I actually knew about the subject. My junior year, my mom suggested I write my common app college essay about my interest in law, reminding me that I could always call up Ms. Pingly, no matter how many years it had been since her husband taught me.

I wasn't sure I wanted to be a lawyer, but I also wasn't sure I didn't. And I definitely didn't have an alternate idea, especially since my other "choices" didn't appeal to me. So, instead, I continued to act the part, wondering if one day I would wake up and be a lawyer because I forgot to decide I didn't want to.

Often, I wondered why I couldn't just be like my brother, who was only one year younger than me. He decided in middle school that he wanted to be a drummer in a band, despite not playing the drums. No one planned out his aspiring musical career. Instead, he was given the freedom to simply wonder what he wanted to be. Or just not to think about it yet.

"I just don't think I'll get to do something as fun as play professional basketball," I blurted out after a long pause for thinking. I wasn't even sure I thought that sounded fun. I had never excelled in any sport, despite my height and my town's obsession with student athletes. I felt frustrated Piper believed we were all lucky enough to have Adrian's or even her own fate.

"I firmly believe you can make anything fun. And if it isn't, then make it funny." The way she cocked her head made me feel as though she had said that before.

I thought about what she said. I almost felt the need to shake the discomfort out of my arms. Did I do things that were fun?

Piper was looking straight ahead, a slight smile on her face, as if she were remembering a hilarious moment from her past.

I closed my eyes and tried to remember a time I had had fun.

# CHAPTER 6

# THE FEELING
# OF WRITING

———

Fun didn't feel like the right word. No, there was no right word. Other than maybe "feeling," but even that felt too broad, like something others experienced too. And these moments felt like they were mine.

I had grown used to driving around with Shelby, listening to her playlists, "Dance Party," "Songs to Get Drunk To," "Freshman Year 2019." We weren't in college, but Shelby liked to play music she imagined college students listened to, as she fantasized about leaving these suburbs and going off on her own. Her parents weren't strict, only a little stricter than mine, and life in the suburbs didn't feel so bad to me, but I didn't shoot down her dreams. I just hummed along to the songs on her carefully curated playlists.

When Shelby and I stopped hanging out, I just couldn't seem to write, so my time spent in the car only increased. I told my mom I was at the bookstore because I wasn't sure she would understand my constant driving around. Whenever I wanted to do an activity she didn't enjoy, even if it was just driving or spending time by myself in my room writing, she believed these to be signs of mental turmoil. I had never had a mental breakdown, but she sat on the proverbial edge of her chair waiting for the rite of passage so she could guide me through the challenges of becoming an adult.

If anything, my car rides were quite the opposite.

I started out just driving the roads Shelby and I knew. When I first got my license, Shelby pulled out our school directory and looked up all the addresses of people in our grade. We felt like the only two students without sports practice after school, so as the bells rang and our peers poured out of the schoolhouse and onto their designated fields, we hopped into my family's car and wound our way through neighborhoods. Stone walls kept in goldendoodles but did nothing for our prying eyes and curious minds as we drove past our classmates' houses and commented on what we knew about them. Thinking about it retrospectively, I cringed at how creepy it seemed, but in the moment, it really was just something to do. Somewhere to go that made us feel like we weren't standing still.

Together, we imagined our classmates in their McMansions with stone facades or their ivy-covered brick estate homes, practicing the cello, fighting with a sibling, applying to college. While I felt like Shelby wondered what these people did, I wondered who they were. Were the squeaking cello strings sirens calling out for easier paths to success? Were screaming matches warnings of intergenerational mistakes being repeated? Were futures decided by a single moment in a sports game, only to be replayed over and over within the enclaves of their family rooms?

I now realized that to her these were people we knew tangentially from school, while to me they were characters in a story.

Without Shelby there, I drove a little slower, my eyes covering the suburban landscape on both sides of the street. Sometimes I'd even pull over, faking a phone call or pretending to check maps for directions as I waited for an elderly couple to pass on foot or for a lone child on a scooter to cross the street. Then, I'd snap a picture of a shiny new car's wheels, a weather-worn mailbox pole, a historic old home becoming a shiny mansion. I found myself incorporating these pieces into the stories I wrote, uncovering what these details may say about the lives of the people who owned the images I carried around on my phone.

Once I had snaked through every neighborhood, passed every private winding driveway, and turned at every cul-de-sac along Shelby's and my various routes, I altered my path. I ventured to the other side of downtown in the direction of the water. Suburbia became coastal as I made my way down the singular roads on the peninsulas jutting off the mainland. Each house told its own story, red-roofed farm-style homes, mammoth stone chateaus with green awnings, and beachy wood-planked mid-century structures with wide windows looking out into the world.

I opted out of the GPS until it was time to drive home, though with the dead ends and patchwork suburban streets, I never found myself very far adrift.

Without Shelby and my writing, the two things that filled my time, driving occupied my afternoons and weekends. While I told myself I liked listening to music, pop melodies that blurred together, I knew it was the freedom to observe, to see into the most personal spaces of people's lives, that I craved. Alone in the car, nothing in the reality of my life competed for my attention. Here, I lived inside my head.

As the beats rose, the console in our family's Lexus vibrated, reverberating around the space only I occupied. In these moments, I would think about my characters. And I loved them. These people I created, each of them complex and unique. Each with their own story, as if they were friends of mine. Friends who didn't judge me, who didn't cause me to worry because I was in control of their futures. They could be anyone I wanted them to be.

A smile stretched across my face, and I watched cars driving past me. Did they think I lived here too? That they and I belonged in the same spaces? I eyed the mansions around me and wondered if the people in the cars worried I knew something intimate about them. I knew they were unable to discern the features of my face through my closed windows. But they could see my motions. I wondered if they saw me the same way I would look at them, laughing with their friends or on stage unabashedly showing the world who they were. I wondered if they saw me and smiled. Or if they saw me and felt even more alone, the car windows a chasm between their world and mine.

Because that's what it was. A safeguard and a curse. And my writing allowed me to cross that void, to understand these strangers around me, without the pain or joy of really letting someone in.

So was writing fun? I wasn't sure. But it sure was something.

## CHAPTER 7

# STORYTELLING AND STAND-UP

---

"What do *you* do for fun?" I asked Piper. By the broad smile across her face, I was certain the answer would not likely be a bonding experience between us.

"I thought you'd never ask!" she exclaimed dramatically, holding the back of her hand to her forehead, as if waiting for this question caused her to feel faint or nauseated. A response that smacked of overkill in my opinion.

"Comedy!" she said, fanning herself with her hand. "Why'd you think I was here? Did ya know we might even get to meet Gad?"

Stand-up comedians seemed like an odd representation of God, I thought, but maybe I misheard her. I would only later come to understand her allusion to the comedian Gad Elmaleh. "Sorry," I said, "I should have made the connection."

I realized why she had been so pressed to know what brought me here. She wanted to talk comedy, and I had admitted that comedy played no factor in my decision to volunteer.

I regretted not asking her what brought her to volunteer at the festival earlier.

"No worries, I just really thought I'd get some sweet gig ushering comedians to the stage or at least monitoring the concert halls and getting to hear some sets." Her arms splayed out at this dreary setup, which included me.

I felt self-conscious by what a disappointment sitting with me was. "Yeah, that probably would be a lot more fun. Sorry."

She turned to me. "Don't apologize so much. That's dumb."

I had to hold my tongue not to apologize for being dumb.

"Adrian's volunteering too," she said, making a gesture to indicate that he was out there somewhere. And I tried to imagine her relationship with him. Did she wonder if he got a better position? Did she wish they could have volunteered together? Or did she cherish the time they had apart? Instead, I asked her if Adrian did comedy.

"Nope but he sure does do comedians." She cackled; this was becoming a theme with her.

I laughed but didn't know how to respond. I waited until she was quiet before clarifying that I was asking about his interest in comedy, since he was a volunteer as well.

She smiled, and the rosiness that came to her cheeks made me smile too. "No, he's just volunteering to get us more of a chance at winning the raffle. Well, at giving me more of a chance of winning the raffle, since I think he knows I couldn't take him if we won something really cool. My comedian friends would murder me."

"Wow, that's really nice of him," I said and wondered how differently my night would have gone if I had been paired with Adrian. Maybe I'd hear all about Piper.

"Mmhmm," she hummed. Just as she smacked her lips, we heard the booming voice of the cannon man. It must have been 7:30. Even with the distance and his thick accent, I could hear the echo of his voice over the crowd. As he prepared for the performance, hyping up the audience, I wondered how far we were from my family's rented apartment. For all I knew, I had walked in a full circle around the perimeter of the festival as I searched for the volunteer van. Or, perhaps, I had walked to the far end of the festival and the guide had walked me right back to where I started.

My mind was not on how I would get home; it was on my parents in the apartment watching coverage of the festival. It was about the thousands of people, maybe hundreds of thousands of people throughout the city, all hearing the cannon man go boom.

We sat in silence, letting the performance run its course, and I didn't speak again until I heard the cheers from the crowd. Still thinking about the cannon man, I asked her what kind of comedy she was into.

"Oh, man, I love all comedy but stand-up and improv are what I love to do." Piper's enthusiasm made me immediately regret telling her I had never been to a comedy show, since we were, as she reminded me, at the world's largest comedy festival.

"I live with my parents," I said a bit too defensively. "I'm not even sure where you'd find a comedy show in the suburbs where I live."

"You don't need to find a traditional comedy show to find people who are funny," she quipped with teasing sarcasm. "Some of my best nights have been at open mic nights at bars, staying until the final 2 a.m. performances, which are not in the least bit funny but that doesn't matter since everyone is drunk." Piper added, "Of course, I don't drink, but I like to be surrounded by people who are laughing."

I didn't remind Piper that I was seventeen and had never been to a bar. I thought about how my mom loved to cite research studies. She'd say, "The research shows that the drunker you get, the funnier you feel. But the feeling is not shared by others." *How would she respond to Piper?*

"The end of my first year at university, after I moved to Canada, I really started getting into these bars," she said and added, "I think I was about your age." I thought about asking her what university she went to but was afraid I wouldn't catch the name of it having barely heard of schools outside the US. Piper frowned, "My classmates were God awful."

I must have made a questioning expression.

"I'm not kidding," she said. "All the education majors dressed like they were their own mothers, or their mother's mother." Her tone didn't match the words. "And they wanted to mother me. As if!" Again, the sarcasm but Piper didn't really seem offended, just amused, like she was thinking about all the "your mamma jokes" she could use.

I felt like education majors sounded like the perfect welcoming party. They wanted to nurture her, to welcome her to Canada with well-intentioned advice.

"My mother is not that bad a dresser," I said, hoping she would see I was following her and so she would explain herself a bit more.

She exhaled. "Man, it's been decades since I took my degree, and it still feels good to complain about wanna-be teachers." She added in a more reassuring tone, "I get a lot of laughs from teacher jokes. Everybody's had teachers and everybody has hated 'em."

I laughed more so at her use of hyperbole. There was no way it had been decades since Piper had been my age. She did not act like she'd been an adult for very long at all.

I wanted to ask what was so wrong with people being nice, especially since she said that it had taken almost a year after her arrival in Canada before she ventured out to a bar near her apartment.

"Before getting into comedy, I didn't really go to bars," Piper began. "But two couples who lived down the hall in my apartment building invited me to tag along with them. And honestly, it wasn't like I had anything else going on."

"It was April," Piper said, glancing off into the distance. "It was warm enough to walk to the bar. Zach, a guy in the group who liked to make decisions, picked a table in the center of the room, electing Sarah, his girlfriend, to go to the bar and try to get everyone free drinks." Piper shrugged. "The evening started out nothing special. Everyone had a few drinks, and, well, I had a few sips." She made a face as if she still remembered the taste of cheap beer 20 years later.

I liked listening to Piper's story. She went on to explain how from their vantage point in the bar, an enormously tall man stood at the back by the bathrooms. Her group began pointing at him, and Piper noticed other people around her murmuring. It seemed rather rude to her, until she perked her head up and realized he was standing on a platform and was gripping a mic in his hand. While some people in the room had quieted down, his calls for attention were in vain. Piper was skeptical, not knowing whether this was an entertainment venue, not in the mood for whatever the man might want and thinking about making her way home. Was he going to ask for money or something?

"Hey, you there," the man shouted in Piper's direction.

Piper's group went completely silent and looked excitedly at her.

"You!"

Piper motioned to herself with an inquisitive glare.

"Yes, you," he shouted, as if to rile her up. He paused for a moment, giving the crowd time to process what he was saying. "You look like you're trying to take a massive shit, but you're not smart enough to figure out how to do it."

At this, the room went silent and turned to look and see if Piper was in fact a pooping idiot. After a moment, she burst into laughter and turned to give him her full focus. *Ahhhh,* she thought. *So he's a comedian.* From up there on stage, he didn't care that she was new to Canada. He didn't care that she had left behind everyone she knew and loved. All he cared about was making her laugh at this very moment. Piper knew the feeling.

He introduced himself and went on to perform a comedy sketch that barely scraped the bar of mediocrity. The few laughs he got were mostly from Piper, and five minutes later, he was off the stage, replaced by a slightly funnier guy. After six comedians, all male, had rotated on and off the stage, Piper's friends decided to go back to their apartment building for a nightcap. Piper let them leave without her and stayed to watch another sketch.

Thirty minutes later, the funniest guy of the night climbed off the stage, and Piper rushed over to insist on buying him a beer.

I wasn't sure where this story was going, but as it turned out, Piper wasn't into the guy. She was into his comedy. She bought him a drink and then another, asking him how he came to be so funny. Of course, he was not a full-time comedian, or he would be in very bad shape financially, but he knew enough about the comedy scene in Montreal to tell Piper where to go for the good stuff.

But Piper didn't care about the good stuff. Instead, she spent the rest of the year going to poorly attended comedy shows and open mic nights, buying comedians beers. She began taking a notebook with her, jotting down what kinds of jokes hit and which ones didn't. Instead of watching the comedians, she would watch the crowd. She ignored the people who seemed determined not to laugh. They weren't worth it, drunk or sober.

I admired her ability to filter out critics. It was one thing for me to fear that a single anonymous individual who I would never meet wouldn't like my writing. It was another thing to stand up on stage and watch people who don't like you or what you do. Maybe it was easier for her to handle because she too got to be a critic.

I thought about what it would be like to go up to the strangers I had a habit of wondering about. What would it be like to ask them about their lives, why they made decisions I watched them make, and who were they as people? But Piper seemed more interested in learning from these people than she was in learning about them.

"Wait. Do you ever perform yourself?" I asked. I tried to picture Piper up on a stage in the glow of a spotlight.

Her eyes lit up at the question, and she launched into a memory. It had been over a year since she'd been attending comedy shows. She would trek across the city to go to the Red Boot, a bar where anyone could go up on stage and perform anything they wanted. Most people sang poorly. Some played piano, which was even more painful to hear given that the piano was out of tune. Her favorite performers did comedy, of course. The audience was always too drunk to care about what was happening on stage because few showed up at the Red Boot until around 1 a.m. when the restaurants were closing. Each weekend, Piper went, waiting for a sign.

And then one day, the stage was empty. Piper hadn't planned to do it that evening, but she never really planned on getting up on stage at all. It was a warm summer night, and she didn't know anyone in the room. She looked up at that empty stage, the microphone dangling over its stand, drooping toward the ground. Her horoscope from that morning suggested that instead of shying away from new things, she should move forward with them. Sweat beaded on her forehead, but when she looked out at the crowd and everyone was piss drunk and focused on their own night, she moved through the tables and climbed up on stage.

She didn't remember actually getting there, picking up the microphone, and walking to the front of the stage. In fact, she didn't remember most of the sketch.

She just remembered opening with, "So my dad died." The crowd quieted, probably realizing it was bad karma to make out with strangers or take tequila shots while someone talked about the death of a family member. "Oh, no need to look at me that way. He wanted to."

A few people smiled, but then seemed to feel awkward for smiling. The rest was a blur, recounting stories about her dad from when he was alive. About her brothers sneaking into the fridge and gutting the four oranges her parents got for the kids, surgically applying the peels to bouncy balls and placing them back in the fridge like nothing happened. She made fun of the teachers at her school and even more so made fun of herself.

At one point, she had members of the audience raise their hands if they were immigrants, and while she had been reminded over and over how Toronto was a melting pot, she didn't truly feel it until that night. And she felt much less lonely.

While Piper talked, I could feel the excitement of her indoctrination into the world of comedy. Finally making friends, and more importantly, finding people whom she could make laugh. I asked her questions about the people she'd met, the venues she'd performed at. I listened, nodding along with her reminiscences.

Her words wove themselves into a world that was both familiar and yet completely new to me. I didn't want her to stop talking about it. Unsure of comedy lingo, I asked her which kinds of jokes she liked to tell.

Piper took a long pause, her eyes focused on the cement wall behind me. "They're not so much jokes as they are stories. I'd say I'm a storytelling kind of comic. Or the self-deprecating type, but only because I know I'm awesome." She smiled.

"Huh. I hadn't thought about jokes that way. Though I guess most of my exposure to jokes had been through the lame ones my mom tells. Like, she thinks she's the first person to ever yell at her daughter for not wearing pants just because they're camo. Camouflage, get it?"

She chuckled. "Yeah, couldn't promise you that would land with these crowds. Don't be fooled by the fact that they're Canadians. They definitely can be tough." She looked like she was remembering a bad show, but with a quick shake of her head, her smile returned.

We sat in silence for a moment, and I hadn't planned on saying it, but the words just slipped out of my mouth. "I think I might be a storyteller too."

"Is that so?" Piper seemed to like my response. "Tell me a story," she said as if egging me on.

I wracked my brain for my favorite story. No, not my favorite story, a story Piper would like. There was a large difference between my favorite story and my favorite conversation.

Some fabulous conversations were challenging to actualize into a story. Mundane conversations could make the most spectacular stories.

I considered a conversation I had overheard between three women who were out to lunch at Panera Bread Company. They all appeared to be in their mid-eighties, at least. My mom and I ate in silence as I strained my ears to make out some pieces of wisdom. Instead, I overheard them shit talking Delores, another woman from their retirement community. As it turns out, they lied to her about where they had gone, not wanting to invite her to their weekly lunch. They mimicked her with a nastiness I thought only high schoolers were capable of. In some ways, the conversation was upsetting, as it dawned on me that there was no escape from the vapidity and rejection of others. And yet there was a certain level of comfort knowing things could always stay the same. Everyone around me had changed so rapidly from who they were in elementary or middle school. Maybe the entropy was over.

I could already hear Piper's dissent. Her claims that at any moment I could pick up and change my life entirely. That the entropy must go on. So instead, I settled on telling her about a conversation I overheard between an older man and a twenty-something hipster. I thought Piper may be able to help me untangle at least a little of the absurdity. I wondered what kind of story it would become, since the more interesting of the two characters remained entirely a mystery to me. I just could not understand the motivation or rationale for his behavior.

I started my story with the setting. "I was at Whole Foods with my mom," I said. "And she had sent me to grab frozen vegetables on the other side of the store. While looking for the largest bag of frozen corn I could find, I noticed a young guy whose arms overflowed with all sorts of pre-made frozen meals, pizzas, and sides. Why he had not grabbed a basket at the entrance of the store was beyond me." I shook my head in disapproval to emphasize that this fact was integral to the story. "He had a watch on, but it was a small analogue one, and I noticed him struggling to turn his wrist to check the time without dropping any of the many items he held. And he looked cold. I considered pulling out my phone and giving him the time."

"An old man stood next to him, holding a basket with nothing but a pre-stuffed Cornish hen. The young man turned to the old man and said, 'Sir, do you know what time it is?' The old man looked down at his own wrist and without reacting said, '4:37.'"

"The young man's face dropped and he practically sprinted out of the frozen food aisle. I was also surprised by the time. I searched more urgently for the corn, when I heard the old man chuckle to himself as he selected a pint of Half Baked Ben and Jerry's ice cream. I almost thought I imagined it," I said. "From down the aisle, I heard him mutter, 'Dumbass.'" I paused a moment to allow Piper to wonder why.

"I pulled out my phone and saw it was only 3:30. I found the corn and returned to my mom, who was at the butcher's station."

"Ha!" Piper threw her head back, "I love it. People who lie for absolutely no reason are the best."

I wholeheartedly disagreed with her, but maybe she didn't mean that pathological liars made the best partners, friends, doctors, or teachers. No, they made the best stories. I thought about that for a moment; the unreliable narrator was one of my favorites. Not one who blatantly lied though, simply one who saw the world through the lens of her own partiality, often unaware that the truth was clouded.

Maybe that was the difference between Piper's and my stories. Hers showed the absurdity, mine sought to comprehend it. And maybe, just maybe, not everything is that deep.

Piper was still smiling at the idea of the old man's trickery. "I hope I still have that much fun when I'm super old." She became even more animated. "Mind if I use that in a sketch?"

I nodded at her and was glad I hadn't told the story about the catty lunch table of octogenarians.

"You are a storyteller, Violet. Like, you really told that story." She spoke so emphatically, I almost believed her.

# CHAPTER 8

# MEETING A MINION

---

Despite our storytelling similarities, unlike me, Piper was out-in-the-open visible. On stage in front of a crowd, she was identified as the source of her story. Even just imagining myself on a stage made me shudder. The awkwardness of a crowd of people looking at me, no matter how drunk or unfocused, made me want to shrink into an invisible version of myself.

I considered asking Piper how she got so brave but, instead, I continued to sit in a silence she didn't seem to mind.

She sat with her legs stretched out straight in front of her, only ankles crossed. Her shoulders were relaxed, and she allowed them to occupy space; her hands met in her lap. Everything about her stature reminded me that she wasn't thinking too hard about it. Meanwhile, I sat next to her, back bent forward, one knee clenched tightly over the other, my crossed arms resting in my lap. I tried to un-pretzel myself a little, mimicking her relaxed arms but keeping my legs crossed.

I was so focused on Piper's positioning that I didn't notice the frantic young man sprinting toward us until he was practically entering our space. I jumped, but Piper kept her cool.

The man didn't look dangerous, but he also didn't look like a street performer. He hardly slowed as he made his way around us, choosing the open pathway between me and the wall rather than prying the two of us apart and potentially knocking us over. He flung open the doors behind us, and we, clearly bad at our jobs, merely watched him as he entered and continued on. We were able to see his silhouette as he ran down the hallway, until the doors behind us fell shut again.

"Eh, he looks like he knows where he's going. Probably all good, right?" Piper's question only had one answer.

"Yeah, probably, I think." My heart was racing from the momentary intrusion, unable to make a quick decision whether to ask him who he was, if he had permission to be in the building, or for some form of ID. I was glad that Piper had frozen too, even if her disregard was from indifference, not anxiety.

Before she could respond, the man burst through the doors again. If we had positioned our chairs a foot farther back, we would have been unwitting victims of the heavy double doors.

Instead of running past us, the man made his way around my chair again. Only this time, he approached and faced us head on. "*Est-ce que vous pouvez m'aider?*" he asked, his eyebrows rising in desperation.

I was about to ask what he needed help with when he motioned to a giant yellow blob of fabric tucked under his arm. He checked his watch on his other forearm, almost dropping his parcel.

"*Putain, vingt heure. Merde je suis toujours en retard,*" he cursed.

I glanced at my phone. *Late for what?* Then I realized he was probably supposed to start his shift at 8:00 and wasn't ready for it yet. I felt a tinge of empathy.

Before we could offer our help, to our surprise, he stripped off his shirt, revealing the abs of a very skinny twenty-something. In an attempt to reclaim some decency, he turned around, his bare backside facing us. He threw the yellow blob over his head and turned back around. Neither Piper nor I had moved other than to stand up. Instead of the frantic man facing us, we were staring straight into the single eye of a polyester minion. Piper and I discreetly grinned at each other before I noticed the zippers the minion was trying to grab hold of with his long foam fingers. Piper and I approached either side of him and zipped up the costume, completing this man's transformation into a giant yellow circle with one eye, a wire curl sticking out of the top of his head, and brown sneakers protruding out from the bottom.

"*Merci beaucoup!*" he shouted as he waddled out the door and into the festival.

"Well, glad he wasn't homeless," Piper said, shrugging. "He was pretty cute, what'd you think?"

I blushed. He wasn't out of the alleyway yet, likely not even out of earshot, but it was hard to tell. "A bit old for me," I said.

"How old are you, again?"

"Seventeen." I considered reaching for my phone to take a picture of his silhouette, imagining a story that could come from this scene had I decided to start writing again. I debated whether I would include the swear word in the story, even if it was in French. I didn't necessarily try to keep my writing PG, but swears felt so heavy and awkward. Like the sentence wasn't made to include them, and they were plopped in to sound cool. Nevertheless, there was nothing natural about a minion dropping the French equivalent to the F bomb.

The minion rounded the corner and was lost from sight.

Piper chucked, "That would not have been my response at seventeen."

Already uncomfortable, I let out a "mmhm," the corners of my mouth curving up ever so slightly.

"Though can't say I would have done anything about it." She sighed, shaking her head, as if remembering high school crushes on older men.

"I get that, the not doing anything about it, I mean, not the older men part." I stumbled over my words.

"I thought you would. You give me that vibe," Piper said. I must have made a face because she immediately explained, "You seem shy, I mean. Don't look offended, I was that way too so no judgment."

Now surprised, I used her words, "Really? You actually don't give me that vibe."

"Well, I'm old now!" She chuckled, "But it took me years to get over myself."

Piper's eyes were glued to a small weed growing out of the cracks in the cement just outside our space. She was hyper-focused; it was hard to believe she couldn't will the plant to grow. I thought about what she had said, that she had managed to get over her shyness. I didn't think I'd be so lucky. I always struggled to imagine myself any older than I was in that moment, but one thing I never saw changing was the cruel voice inside my head.

When Shelby and I were still friends, I lingered in the hallway after she and I parted ways every day after lunch; during our junior year, she had a free period while I was in history, and we would reconnect for last period English. The way the schedules worked, we had half our classes together and then half our classes with different groups of students. Before entering the history classroom, I would wait by the water fountain to fill up my water bottle, knowing my seat in the classroom was safe because everyone always sat in the same seats. The other kids with a free period after lunch embraced Shelby; many were a part of the "Dream Fifteen." When they cruelly defined the high school hierarchy even more by naming themselves, I pointed out to Shelby that dream and fifteen didn't even rhyme. Her honorary membership as the sixteenth member of the group didn't prevent her from laughing at this oversight with me.

Shelby's locker wasn't near mine. That's not how things worked at our school. Instead, Maplewood High School chose to torture its students with the cubby grab. We had lockers like any other public high school, but to mask the cruelty of the tradition, they opted to refer to the storage spaces as "cubbies," likening them to the joys of preschool. On the first day of school, students would arrive hours before the first bell, line up outside laughing and sharing stories from their summer vacations and away camps, waiting for the doors to open. When they did, it was a mad dash to claim a locker closest to the senior lounge, even though we were not seniors. It was common knowledge by junior year that the cubbies closest to the senior lounge were where the coolest kids hung out. Coolness radiated out from there. Some students made a statement by arriving early to select the lockers farthest from the senior lounge as a form of teenage rebellion.

I didn't buy into the mad dash or the rebellion. I hadn't even heard of it when I started at Maplewood High School freshman year, but each year I had still managed to get a locker somewhere between the lounge and the school entrance. Shelby begged me to arrive early with her. She even camped out over night before our junior year. I wondered if her parents would let her for senior year. I hoped for her sake that they would. Senior year would be the only year logical enough to care so much about getting a locker by the lounge.

During her free period, Shelby and the other kids with cubbies next to the senior lounge would sit on the floor, their backs against the wood of their cubbies and their legs all scrunched up so they weren't completely blocking the hallway. I could almost see them from the window of the history classroom door but thankfully not quite.

I was glad Shelby had other friends. In some way, it took the pressure off of me. But it also wasn't always easy seeing her having fun with the Dream Fifteen. She and I had some fun together, driving around, talking about the meaning of life, making fun of her parents for being so haphazardly clueless, but it wasn't the same kind of carefree fun she seemed to be able to have with her other friends.

I would remind myself not to think about that and would join my small group in the history classroom. I wouldn't call us friends, but I would say we were a group of five who cared equally about school: a lot. We sat in the second row to the right in the classes we had together: history, math, and art. Jeremy, a lanky messy-haired boy in our little group answered nearly every other question asked by a teacher, which made most teachers ignore the rest of us, as our side of the room had already been represented. Plus, there was an advantage to sitting right behind the front row, because that was occupied by students who had been caught causing trouble.

In January of our junior year, right before midterms, I found my mind wandering away from Ms. Caren's review session on the Industrial Revolution and onto the text conversation on the laptop of the boy in front of me. I could barely make out the recipient of his texts, but my guess was confirmed when I saw his friend from across the room furiously typing back. The intensity was directed at their important debate: where did Ms. Caren rank on a scale from 1-10? Despite both boys coming to the agreement that she was hot for someone old enough to be their mom, I was upset by the conversation. My eyes returned to Ms. Caren, not taking in what she was saying, rather feeling empathy that while she was explaining something she cared about, at least two students were now sexualizing her. Naturally, with my eyes following Ms. Caren across the room, she paused to ask me a question about the reading.

I stared at her, my heart racing. I admired Ms. Caren, and even hoped she would write one of my college letters of recommendation. Before I could stammer out that I hadn't heard the question, Jeremy's nasally voice informed her that I had made a brilliant point answering that exact question when we had been in discussion circles earlier that class. Rather than reprimanding me for not answering the question, Ms. Caren acknowledged that it was a good point and moved on to the next question. Jeremy had not made up my point, but he had certainly exaggerated its brilliance in front of the class. I mouthed a thank you to him, wondering why someone would put themselves out there when they didn't need to, especially since he and I were hardly friends.

After class, Jeremy followed me out, complimenting my point yet again. He was one of the only boys in our grade who was taller than me yet not an athlete. I looked up at him, and he rattled on about history, which was his favorite subject. When he was finished, it was almost time for our next class. Luckily, the English classroom was on the same hall as history. Jeremy, on the other hand, had to run across the school's campus to get to biology.

I stopped by my cubby to get my *Jane Eyre* book for English. When I shut the locker door, Shelby's face was split in a huge grin. "Was that Jeremy?" she asked. She knew it was. "Yeah," I said. "He's in my other classes. Why?"

"I know something you don't know," she practically sang, and I was surprised she hadn't already texted me.

I could see where this was going and before she continued, I began walking to English. She skipped alongside me, "I heard something about Jeremy." She emphasized each syllable in his name. It was clear she wanted me to ask what she had heard, but instead, I just tried to focus on not walking weirdly. Did people usually swing their arms? And why did my legs feel uneven?

"Violet, he likes you!" she said, as if it was the best news I could possibly have heard. Though from one look at my expression, she realized this attraction was not reciprocated. I never found myself thinking about love, much less potential love interests. All I could think was how incredibly awkward the whole situation was. To make things worse, Shelby knew. She wasn't friends with Jeremy, so if she had heard this information, chances were a lot of others had too.

"Shelby, who told you that?" I asked urgently.

"Oh, it was sent in the Dream group chat. I think Sara sent it, but also Josh confirmed it," she said.

She spoke liberally about the Dream group chat, a text chain that Shelby was included in and I was not. And in that moment, I was so glad I wasn't.

She pushed, as we sat down in our seats for English. The bell had not rung yet, and she spoke with a sense of desperation, as if this were a matter we had to figure out before English started or any chance of love would be lost. I reminded her that I didn't want a boyfriend. She didn't either, despite the rotation of boys on the lacrosse team who asked her out. I felt a twinge of frustration that Shelby thought she was too good for some of the best athletes in our state, but that I should date Jeremy, the only seventeen-year-old obsessed with World War I. I didn't say this though, because as soon as I thought it, I wanted to kick myself. Why did I think *I* was too good for Jeremy? No, that wasn't it.

I told Shelby that I needed to focus on school and that second semester junior year wasn't a good time to start a relationship because it was bound to end when we went off to different colleges. Within a minute, I was saved by the bell, and Mr. Abel began his reading from a book of poems, a class tradition to get us in the English mood. Instead of listening to his tenor voice recite a monologue, I imagined Jeremy sending a text to Michael, another boy in our class, pondering whether I was attractive enough to date. And then Jeremy deciding something about me was worth talking about at his lunch table. And the people at lunch thinking, "Who is that girl?" And talking about how Jeremy might get a girlfriend. And wondering if I would say yes if he asked me out. And deciding they better ask Simon because he was friends with Shelby who was friends with me. And before anyone knew it, at least five people had spoken about me, wondered what I would be like as a girlfriend, pondered if I was attractive, asked Jeremy if he was sure he liked me, and looked me up on social media. I tried not to hyperventilate.

Instead of letting Jeremy ask me out and me either saying yes or no, the following day I moved to an empty chair on the other side of the history classroom. Nobody said anything. We were allowed to sit anywhere. The kids around me cared slightly less about school but at least no one liked me. Jeremy seemed to get the message. It wasn't as though we talked all the time, but after I switched seats, he never spoke to me unless we were put in the same discussion group. He also avoided walking out of the classroom with me. In fact, he avoided me altogether. Shelby said he felt embarrassed that I had moved on account of him, which only made me feel worse.

Later on, I would wish I hadn't ended my friendship with Jeremy over the hypothetical. Not when other friendships would end over something more than my own stubbornness and rigidity. I would yearn for the comfort of a friend to sit with, even if it was just to do homework together. Jeremy had been interested in me for my ideas. When we talked, he made me feel like my ideas were clever, and I felt the same about how he read the textbook and brought in reading he had done outside of our assigned homework.

I didn't really want to tell Piper about Jeremy. Even just remembering what happened, I knew the whole thing was my fault. All I needed to do was tell Shelby, who could tell her source, who could tell Jeremy's friend, that I didn't want to date him. And that would have been it. We could have still remained friends. If I had learned anything from the Jeremy incident, I might not have lost Shelby too. I didn't want Piper to tell me what I already knew.

At the end of the alleyway, I watched the minion turn around and run in the opposite direction. I could have told him that turning right would only lead him to administrative offices, totally the wrong direction if he wanted an audience and tips. I laughed ever so slightly.

Piper chuckled at the sight too, suggesting, "You could go help him." She winked. Shelby would have said the exact same thing.

I smiled at the thought, even though I could feel my stomach gnaw at itself. Piper smiled too.

"Oh, not you too," I mustered playfully and rolled my eyes. "My best friend's always trying to get me to date someone." It was easier to call her that. Ex-best friend sounded so dramatic. Ex-boyfriend was a badge of honor. Ex-friend meant something was wrong with you.

"Hey, it's always nice to have a wing-woman," Piper said nonchalantly.

"I guess. I kind of don't want one though," I responded, not sure why I was telling her this. But since Shelby was my only real friend, I had never really talked to anyone about her. "It's kind of annoying sometimes."

"Yeah, friends can be that way." Piper hadn't said much about her friends, but she seemed to be unbothered by the fact that her friends were annoying too. "We just have to love them anyway and know the annoying stuff doesn't matter in the end."

My throat tightened at her words. I knew she was right, and yet I had let betrayal, guilt, and awkwardness seep into my mind until I couldn't bear to be around the person I had cared for the most. I don't know why, and I didn't plan it, but everything just poured out.

# CHAPTER 9

# SHELBY'S STORY

———

From elementary school through middle school, I spent all my time with the same group of three friends. As everyone else matured around us, we clung close in our little bubble of childhood innocence, acting out stories outside and berating our younger brothers, who were all more or less the same age. But as our middle school and other middle schools filtered together into a single, large high school, Charlotte moved away, Rebecca switched to private school, and Sara started dressing promiscuously and hanging out with a crowd you would never find in an AP class. So I arrived in ninth grade, terrified and unconvinced by the media that repeatedly told me how incredible and transformative high school would be. I didn't want to transform.

I rambled on, even though the backstory of my life was not needed or interesting. Piper listened patiently, allowing me to weave through childhood anecdotes about my friendships prior to Shelby. She nodded at all the right moments and asked no questions. When I came to a silent pause, there was nothing to do but keep going.

It felt strange to recount my own feelings and experiences, especially out loud. For some reason, I felt a certain level of urgency creep up in my throat, as though this story had been trying to wrestle its way out.

I resisted the urge to get straight to junior year, beginning the story from the beginning. On my first day of high school, I had been looking forward to English, which I had last period. This year, we got to choose our summer reading books from a list. I had chosen John Green's newest book, *Turtles All the Way Down*. I knew it wasn't the most sophisticated choice, but I had lots to say about it. I knew I would only get some of it out in class, always careful not to monopolize the discussion, but I would be more than prepared for our first essay.

Our teacher put us into groups with other students who chose the same books. I got paired up with Shelby, a petite girl from a different middle school, who was seated at the back of the classroom. I walked down the aisle of desks to join her, assuming her choice of seat meant that she wouldn't be willing to move to where I was. I assumed it also meant that this conversation would be intellectually limited. But as I sat down, taking in her translucent skin and practically white hair, she was immediately loquacious and somewhat unique in her opinions, which were both emotionally charged and critically intriguing. She made me think. She argued that the friendship between Daisy and Aza was complex and satisfying. I didn't agree with her, but she spoke so confidently and her eyes grew wide as she raved about how she was Daisy, the fearless detective, looking for her Aza to nurture and protect. I nodded my head. And at the end of the discussion, we had fully fleshed out her ideas. When she offered for us to eat lunch together, I was surprised she didn't already have a better option, and I immediately took her up on it.

From then on, lunch was our tradition. I knew she was turning down a seat at the lunch table where the Dream

Fifteen was beginning to form, yet she would always gesture to me and we would take our lunches to an empty English classroom and eat our sandwiches as she talked about fights with her grandmother who lived with her, countries in Europe she planned to travel to when we graduated, secret conversations with her brother who had run away from home and was now training to be a craftsman in Colorado.

By tenth grade, Shelby was no longer eating sandwiches, and the stories transitioned to which boys liked her and what she was going to wear to homecoming. She decided to go with no date at all because the choice was too hard. I accompanied her, also with no date. During lunches in eleventh grade, she would beg me to join her at parties. She always seemed to have an invite, even though she spent her time at school with me. I wondered if there were lunchroom speculations about why on earth Shelby would choose to spend her lunch time with me. Was I tutoring her in AP English? Were our moms friends? Then I realized that there was no way they were talking about me. Shelby just did what she felt like, and everyone accepted it.

Shelby's life was even more interesting than the stories I read or thought up in my head. And I was her confidante. But while she was giving up her lunch seat to eat with me, it never crossed my mind that I too was giving up a lunch seat next to a stranger who could have become my friend.

Before I got my license, Shelby and I would walk around the small downtown of the suburb where we lived and which she hated. I didn't tell her I secretly loved it. We'd stop and get diet sodas at CVS or açai at Playa Bowls. She'd roll her eyes at the boy's lacrosse roster that hung on storefront windows and we'd pretend we could afford with pocket change the multi-hundred dollar dresses that hung in storefront windows. Shelby would look around and remind me how white everyone was. And I would feel bad for loving home so much but agree with her anyway.

I paused, worried Piper would judge me for this. But she smiled knowingly, and I felt like maybe she understood.

It was home. The only place I had ever lived, and as I thought about it, I recalled memories of going to the candy shop with my brother, when we both became excited about the same thing: sugar. Or the movie theater where my parents took us to see *Grand Budapest Hotel* when we were in middle school without knowing it had nudity. I had gotten up to buy popcorn. Piper chuckled at this.

I felt like I could always count on home to look the way it looked and for the people, who rotated through fashions and hairdos, to otherwise stay the same. Shelby saw this reality too, and every few months on our CVS stop, she'd pick up a new hair-dye and we'd spend the evening coloring her fraying, shoulder-length hair.

What Shelby didn't see was that, just because everyone looked the same from the outside, each repping our high school's Blue Wave mascot, didn't mean they weren't all people walking around with unique thoughts and feelings. Maybe they too walked around in the shadows of their own Shelby, wishing things would never change. I wondered if she thought differently as these people around us popped up in the stories she read over my shoulder and in all likelihood online.

As Shelby spoke, I'd find my focus drifting to strangers around us. To their chats over coffee or phone calls while walking down the street. I listened to them talk. No one seemed to say what they really thought, but then again, neither did I. It was crazy to me that two people could be sitting across from each other in a cafe, thinking thoughts, having feelings, and choosing to talk about tennis. That's why I liked to watch them. To see who sighed a breath of relief when their counterpart got up and left the table. I'd always try to catch gestures and words that didn't quite match the picture each individual painted of themselves publicly.

Shelby didn't seem to mind, or even notice my split attention. I watched her move her arms emphatically, complaining about a fight with her mom or the six-mile run she planned to go on when she got back home. I wondered what life would be like if we all just acted like ourselves. I was guilty of this too. I spent so much time trying to hold back and not become just like everyone else, but also not to stick out, to really just not be anything at all. I had no idea what would happen if someone washed off the neutral-colored paint I coated myself with and I had to reveal the real me.

Even Shelby, who was congratulated for her authenticity, for being so fun and carefree, was a painted picture of herself. She had stopped eating almost entirely, meticulously waxing off the hair that had begun to cover her body, trying to protect it from its own fragility. She would report fun nights of drinking but somehow couldn't remember the details. She would call me in the middle of the night on the weekend sobbing, but then show up at school on Monday adorned in just enough makeup to cover the dark circles around her eyes. She too didn't really want to let anyone in.

I think it was easier for her to come to me because I wasn't in the world that saw the beautiful picture. I mean, I knew she was beautiful, that she was deep and intricate and hurting so much. But I had no one to tell. So our lunches, constant texting, weekend walks, and after school drives remained safe for both of us.

Until I got pulled out of English class. It was the end of junior year, and we were given the whole period to work on practice essays for our college common applications. I was staring at a blank page, wracking my brain for something interesting about me. But I couldn't think of anything at all interesting about *me*. All I could think of was one of the guys on the soccer team on the phone crying about his B+ on the calc test. Or, the girl in front of me in French who texted her younger brother to let him know their dad wouldn't be home for Easter. That he would probably be away for a while. My surroundings were swimming with interesting people, with interesting lives that they sometimes chose to share with the people closest to them. Or that they kept inside, not realizing how much their faces revealed. But me?

Fifteen minutes had passed, and I continued to stare at the page. I was jealous of my English teacher, who would get to read the inner thoughts, or at least the attempt at impressive inner thoughts, of twenty of my peers. But then the principal's assistant came in the classroom and asked me to come with him.

I had never been to the principal's office. Only the really good kids or the really bad kids got sent there. I took my blank paper with me, I still always wrote on paper, but it dampened in my grip as we walked through the school.

When we arrived, the assistant let me into the principal's office quickly, a kind gesture because waiting would have been agonizing.

"Violet, I'm sorry we're meeting in such unfortunate circumstances, but it is our understanding that you are close with Shelby Parker." The principal didn't wait for me to respond, and I didn't know why he used her last name, given that he knew she was my friend and that there weren't any other

Shelbys at our school. He continued, "She isn't in school today. Do you know where she is?"

Of course, I had noticed Shelby was missing, but she missed school a lot these days. She was always sick. I supposed the not eating weakened her immune system. Her parents were also the kind of parents who, if she faked sick, wouldn't mind.

"Is she not home sick?" My eyes pleaded with him, begging for this to be an adequate response. She hadn't responded to my texts yet that morning, and I thought she was sleeping in or watching a movie under her covers in bed, which was a perfectly normal thing to do. Right?

The principal shook his head. "Her parents said she left this morning to go to school, but she never checked into homeroom. We're not sure if she ever got on the bus. And," he added almost as an afterthought, "she left her cellphone at home on the kitchen counter."

I felt like I was going to be sick. I had worried about Shelby, but we were teenagers. She was going to be okay. My mom said half the girls she worked with had eating disorders or depression. Then again, she worked with a select group of her school's student body. I told the principal I didn't know where Shelby was. I told him what he already knew. When she hadn't texted me back, I tracked her. Her phone said she was at home.

Piper adjusted her chair, breaking a silence I hadn't even realized I caused. She muttered an apology and continued to watch me, allowing me to pause while my throat burned. I wasn't crying, but tears in their ducts threatened to wash the expression of strength from my face. After a few calming breaths and a gentle squeeze on my arm from Piper, I continued. At this point, our chairs were facing each other. We weren't a very convincing blockade against trespassers.

The principal kept me in his office until lunch when my mom arrived. She and I sat together in the waiting room not talking while the principal made phone calls from his office. He had closed his door, but the frantic tone in his voice as he spoke with Shelby's parents permeated through the thin walls. Finally, I asked my mom if she thought Shelby would be okay. She said she did. She didn't ask me any questions, like if I had known Shelby was having a hard time or if we had to be seriously worried about Shelby's life. The thought crossed my mind, but it was too heavy for me to handle.

Eventually, they found Shelby but it wasn't until early evening. She had gotten on the bus that morning but then got off at a random stop on the way to school. There was a park with a stream through it, and she was found sitting by the stream. I could picture her there, her legs folded together, shivering from the March air wrapping itself around her.

Shelby had always used her phone as a crutch. The biggest trouble she had ever been in was when she was caught at school texting under her desk. She was never without her phone. She would never leave it at home, not even by mistake. I wondered if she just felt like giving up.

She was suspended from school for a few days, but it didn't go on her permanent record, and she was forced to get a therapist outside of school. When she and I finally spoke about it later, she played it off as if she was just in the mood to play hooky and have a "tech-free day." It hurt my feelings that she didn't text or call me to let me know she was okay first, but I didn't tell her that because I knew she was hurting too.

The dissolution of our friendship wasn't immediate. Shelby and I still ate lunch together but something about this incident made me unable to write, so I had nothing to share with her. She still chattered on but the content she chose to share with me was what someone would tell an acquaintance. She texted less. And after a few weeks, she had to do a school project during lunch with someone from her history class. She became unavailable after school, since her mom wanted her at home, and besides, her mom tracked her everywhere now, so we couldn't really go driving. Neither of us suggested plans for the weekends, and I'd still see pictures of her at friends' houses pop up occasionally on my phone. Once I even drove past her as she was standing outside The Melting Pot restaurant with a small group, waiting in line to get a table outside. I stopped driving downtown after that.

I swallowed hard. "I imagine this is what heartbreak feels like," I said in a barely audible voice.

Piper seemed like she was about to say something but stopped herself when she saw me continue my thought out loud.

Shelby had just skipped school but my mind reeled to the worst-case scenario, knowing if anything truly terrible had happened, I should have been able to help her. But I didn't. "It just sucks. I feel really bad." I turned my face away from Piper, taking a moment to wipe the corners of my eyes with the t-shirt sleeve.

I hadn't even told my mom the full story about how much I really knew about what was going on with Shelby. Everything she had *not* told me but that I might have subconsciously known anyway. What I then convinced myself I hadn't noticed. I hated myself for that. But I hated myself more when I realized how much I'd missed, my attention absorbed by the table next to us, not the person sitting in front of me.

The minute I'd drawn the connection, I knew I had to stop making up stories about other people. I had spent so much time focused on random people in my classes, the girl who led the debate team, the barista at Starbucks with a nose ring, the old man who talked to his little brown dog while they walked past my house. And not the people I actually knew. For some reason, the stories, the lives of people around me grabbed my attention in a way my own life didn't. I knew a lot of anonymous memoirists online, and they each seemed to have inspiring stories to tell. And all I could do was get lost in daydreams inspired by the small windows I had into people's lives through the words I overheard them speak and those I imagined were left unspoken. All the while, I'd basically ignored what was going on with my closest friend.

Piper sympathized, "It's hard being a teenager."

She made no claim about me being a bad friend, or a good one for that matter.

I could feel my lip quiver and knew Piper noticed.

"It's not your fault about Shelby. That shit happens. I'm surprised you haven't pulled anything like that given how in your own head you are. Though I guess you feel a bit too pulled together to lose your shit like that." She was so matter of fact about it all, as if having a mental breakdown was something that everyone experienced on the daily.

I heard plenty of stories from my mom about the struggles of the kids she helped. Plenty of kids at my school suffered with mental illness. I often wondered if I did, only to snap out of it and realize that was just my self-centeredness talking. With other people, it was stories. With Shelby, it was her reality. "I know it happens, I just never really had to deal with it before. And I don't think I was really there for her."

"It's brutal," Piper admitted. "But it does get easier. In some ways."

# CHAPTER 10

# BUCHAREST, ROMANIA

—

A sound chirped from Piper's back pocket. I instinctively grabbed my phone as well, even though I had been putting it on "do not disturb" since middle school.

While she opened up the text, I appreciated the moment of disregard so I could push my palms along the corners of my eyes again, extracting any tears that had been repressed, vying to escape, as I unloaded my story about Shelby. Why did I share so much personal information? I could only imagine what Piper thought of me now.

While part of me felt regret about sharing so much, another feeling overpowered that discomfort: relief.

Once I was certain my eyes were dry, I glanced at Piper. I was glad she was still hunched over her screen, rapidly typing just about the longest text I had ever seen. And her fingers kept going as a look of amusement crossed over her face. I was too far away to read any of the message, but as I strained my eyes, I saw that I wouldn't have been able to decipher her novel anyway. It wasn't in English or even in French.

In the blink of an eye, she hit send and returned her focus to me.

"What are you snooping for?" she teased. "I'm not talking about you, don't worry."

I flushed, not surprised she had noticed but surprised that she would call me out. If I were to catch someone's prying eyes, I would pretend I hadn't noticed and spare them the embarrassment.

But her expression remained light, and she cracked a smile. "I'm kidding with you. I know you're not snooping. I'm assuming you don't read Romanian."

I smiled back, shrugging my shoulders. "No. Can't say I do."

"Figured, no Americans bother."

She was right. I couldn't argue, so instead, I asked, "Who were you texting?"

"My mom."

"You text that much to your mom?" I asked, unable to mask the shock in my voice. I didn't think my mom had ever gotten that much content out of me face to face while living under the same roof. It was hard to imagine any daughter would send that much in a text to her mom.

"Of course!" Piper exclaimed, raising her eyebrows at the question. "I'm filling her in on boyfriend stuff." She said the last part with a cheeky smile, which made me wonder what kind of details she was telling her mom about her boyfriend.

Unfazed by my bemused expression, she continued, "I tell her everything, even if she doesn't want to hear it…" Her voice trailed off. She smiled, and I considered reassuring her that, of course, her mom wanted to hear everything, but something in her expression made me feel like her statement was truer than she wanted it to be. "That's the beauty of texting," she said. "There's no obvious walking away."

I asked if her mom had ever met Adrian.

"Oh, God, no," Piper scoffed. "I doubt that'll ever happen. Not unless we can somehow make it to Romania together." Her eyebrows perked up. "Ya know, in a way, my mom did set me up with him!" I could tell she was willing that statement to be true. After a pause, she continued, "Well, I guess not exactly, but I wouldn't have met him if it weren't for her."

"Oh, yeah? How'd you guys meet?" I was unfamiliar with my willingness to dive into a conversation about romantic interests.

"Well, my dad's sister, Elena, moved to the US. And she met this woman, Maria, who is also from Romania. Anyway, my mom put me in touch with Elena a few years ago. Then this year, she told Maria, whose thirty-year-old son had just moved to Canada, about me. So they got us set up. And that was, like, four months ago." The way she told the story and talked about Adrian, I was surprised they had only known each other for four months, especially since she had mentioned he lived with her.

She waved her hands about, their motions seemingly disconnected from what she was saying. But with each motion, her bangles chimed, harmonizing with her words.

"So, yeah, I credit my mom and tell her everything, even if she doesn't wanna hear it," Piper said.

I tried to imagine who my mom would set me up with. Probably some athlete who was on student counsel, had lots of friends, and came from a "good" family.

Piper chattered on. "The best part about it being new is that it's still *lots* of fun, if you know what I mean." She made a crude motion. "Gotta thank my momma for that." Her phone lit up with a text response.

I cringed. Thanking her mom for the sex? I wondered if Piper's willingness, even desire, to share everything with her mom was what it was like to be an adult. She was able to have these conversations with her mom because they were two adult friends having adult conversations. Or maybe she was just Piper.

My mom and I just couldn't talk about that kind of stuff, and I reminded Piper that it took a public event for me to even let my mom in about Shelby. And despite that, Piper knew more about what happened than my mom did.

I wasn't sure how to describe our relationship. It was by no means bad. My mom and I fought, but it was never over anything I could pinpoint, anything real. Most recently it was nail polish color, but that felt like nothing compared to what I knew other people went through.

Maybe she actually wanted to sit next to me for more than an hour. Or maybe she wanted to prove that we did mother-daughter things together, things that the troubled teens she worked with always seemed to be missing. Whatever her rationale, my mom had decided we should get mani pedis the first week we were in Montreal.

As we were picking out our choice of polish colors at the salon, she noticed me eyeing a navy so dark it could have been black. "You're not getting black, are you?" she asked.

My cheeks flushed with heat, and I pictured the quizzical look my mom offered Shelby each time she showed up at my house with a different hair color. I had mentally already chosen a nice shade of lilac, "Baguette Me Not," but one look at her disapproving expression and my hand shot out to grab the inky polish.

She compromised, "You can get black on your toes but not on your fingers." She eyed me, knowing she was digging herself deeper into the authority role and that I had no choice but to rebel. She let out a sigh, and I knew she was preparing to concede. But I also knew it was only because she believed that she had this great understanding of my psyche, that she would get to look at my black nails and know that she truly understood her daughter, who simply needed to defy her parents because she was a teenager, not because *I* was an individual.

More embarrassed than actually frustrated, I muttered, "I don't want to do this anymore," and left the salon, despite knowing I had been looking forward to the afternoon.

On my way out, I hoped none of the manicurists had noticed the tears in my eyes. For the moments while my mom tried to figure out what to do in the salon, I considered a breathing technique to lower my heart rate and stop the burning in my throat. But knowing it was she who taught me this technique made me swallow the pain and squeeze my eyes shut.

I didn't want Piper to know I almost cried about nail polish. So I just said, "I think I'm crazy sometimes, especially when I'm talking to my mom," answering no question in particular. "I don't know why. And I feel so awkward about it later."

Piper nodded, her eyes locked with mine. I looked away but felt compelled to keep talking, to clarify what I was trying to say. "I guess something small just happens. I mean, something doesn't even need to happen. But next thing you know, we're yelling at each other or not talking to each other. And then she becomes all calm and rational, as if she understands what I'm feeling. But she can't. And if she can, that's frustrating too."

Piper just nodded again. "You've gotta cut yourself a break here, Violet." Piper spoke with a gentle sternness. "It doesn't have to be that deep all the time."

But I knew it was deeper than that. I thought about my stories. I hated when my mom did to me what I constantly did to others. She was always trying to understand and believed she could simply because she worked with teenagers.

I didn't always want to be understood. I just wanted to be me, to have room to figure out who I was without being watched, without each step I took judged and documented. As if everything I did was building a big puzzle that was me.

The sun had set below the buildings and most of the light came from the single bulb hanging from a wire in our liminal space. Piper let me sit with my thoughts, but I noticed she seemed to be entranced as well. She had mentioned that her dad had died and that her mom still lived back in Romania, but I didn't know anything else about her family.

I let my curiosity get the better of me. "What was it like growing up in Romania?"

She didn't need to think about it. "Oh, it was pretty boring, but *I* wasn't bored because I was too busy laughing."

Piper had twin brothers, and despite actually looking quite different from each other, they maintained identical personalities, or at least to the extent that it mattered to Piper. They were two years younger than her but seemed to think they were two years better. It didn't help that Piper was often lumped in with her sister, who was four years younger than she was. When their father was alive and the family paired up for any sort of game, like the card game Septica, it was always Piper and Daniela. Even after their father passed, Daniela remained Piper's responsibility.

Piper didn't start out so funny. At least that's how she explained it. I couldn't imagine the quiet Piper she described. However, as Piper sketched out her dinner table conversations during her silent phase, I could imagine the experience vividly. The parents asking questions and the brothers' fervent alternating responses, never leaving room for the sisters to get a word in edgewise. But Piper didn't mind; instead, she listened, because she had been blessed with funny brothers.

Piper began to notice how they always answered in stories. It was never, "How was your day?"

"Good. Thanks."

The response was always, "Someone wrote a phone number above one of the urinals with a girl's name after it, and all the boys their year in school went home and immediately prank called the number, leaving messages ranging from demands for 600 chickens to sexual expletives to marriage proposals, and the next day in school, they discovered it was the phone number of one of their math teachers. This was obviously before caller ID hit Romania. The teacher was only able to identify one of the boys, because he, missing the point of a prank call, left his name. He said he called the wrong number, though he never could explain whose child he claimed to be pregnant with." The stories would go on, never about them, even if Piper secretly knew they had been involved in whatever mayhem they described.

"Dinner could take over an hour because no one could find time to eat between laughs," she said with a dreamy look in her eyes. I watched as her expression changed from nostalgic to ruminative. She looked down at her nails, and I let her think in silence.

When she was ready to continue, she explained that when she was fifteen, their father passed away. Their mother took longer shifts at the factory, and everyone's humor got a lot more cynical, except Daniela's, who never had a sense of humor, according to Piper.

They started walking home from school separately, except for her brothers, who remained together continuously. Daniela walked home with a cousin, who was about her age. And Piper walked home alone, wracking her brain for funny things that happened throughout the day to tell her mom. Walking through the door, she was greeted by her brothers' boisterous conversations, ridiculing some European politician or the girls in their grade. Occasionally, they mocked each other, but if that was ever happening when their mom arrived home, it might bring her to tears. So they were more guarded with their mom around.

It didn't take much to bring their mom to tears, and the feat of making her laugh was something Piper began to strive for.

Piper paused again, lost in her memories. She hadn't lifted her eyes from her nails, and she began absentmindedly picking at the skin around her fingers. Shelby did that when she was uncomfortable, so I changed the topic and prodded for more information on Piper's brothers, while eyeing her hands to see if the picking would stop, yet trying not to be caught spying again.

"Despite all their talk, I don't think they had a clue of what was actually going on. Like politics-wise. I mean, they were teenagers and teenagers didn't really care. They just knew they didn't like how things were run, like they didn't like elements of their everyday life, so they would dream up ways of how they would run the country if they were Emil Constantinescu." As she said the name of Romania's president at the time, she rolled her eyes.

Then she went on to list some of their plans, but it was mostly ideas that improved the lives of the fraction of the population that was exactly like them. The stories they told became more cynical, going from prank calls and sex jokes to offhanded comments about military duty or how much or little money their family had. Their pessimism was exhausting.

Piper smiled at me. "Back then, all I could think was 'Would someone just fart or something?'"

I imagined a young Piper, spending all day trying to get together a story, only to arrive home to newly serious brothers, a crying mother, and an eleven-year-old sister, only hoping that her stories would be funny enough. According to her, they rarely were.

*That is why I keep my stories anonymous.* A knowing air of superiority crept over me.

I looked at Piper, and though I was seeing a woman who was almost forty, I tried to imagine her at fifteen. It was hard to picture what she looked like, so in my mind, she looked like a full-figured fifteen-year-old with blue eyeshadow and a school uniform. I wasn't sure she wore one, but it made sense in my head given the rather oppressive cultural climate she described.

I pictured this girl kneeling beside her mother, who lay on the couch, eyes closed but with a bowl of soup resting on her stomach. The young Piper recounted an embarrassing menstruation story while her brothers played chess and pretended not to listen. Her sister remained silent because she didn't fully understand.

And while bleeding through your pants and then being forced to walk to the front of the classroom and answer a math question on the board was undoubtedly funny, her mother barely acknowledged her story, other than to occasionally raise her head and spoon soup into her unsmiling mouth. I pictured Piper as she was in adult form, sending her mother paragraphs of details. Stories about her boyfriend, about her passion for comedy, about her teaching. The screen was now the shield that protected Piper from knowing whether her mom was even listening.

I asked Piper if she journaled. It sounded to me like she would have benefitted from it at that time in her life.

"No," she said, clearly repressing her desire to mock me for my question. "I told stories to make other people laugh," she said instead, explaining why with a derisive laugh. "It's all vanity or self-validation," she insisted. "Who doesn't want people to think they're funny? People like funny people."

This surprised me. I spent exorbitant amounts of time wanting to be liked or at least not noticed enough to be disliked. I tried never to think about all that I could have accomplished if I hadn't wasted time coming up with ways to be a better me on a somewhat superficial level. But Piper? She seemed so confident. Like someone who liked herself enough she didn't care if others did. No, I imagined Piper didn't want people to laugh because she was vain. She wanted them to laugh because she wanted them to be happy. And she was too good of a person to admit that.

I wondered if she recovered some of the satisfaction missing in her childhood now when she made people laugh. I asked her if she made her mom laugh now.

This made her smile. "I like to imagine I do. I mean the shit I send is hilarious, so of course, I do." She paused and said more thoughtfully, "I think things are getting a bit better. Though I wish she weren't alone all the time."

I felt for Piper's mom but knew I could never know what it was like for Piper to be in a country so far from her family home. At least when Piper moved away, she was young and had lots of opportunities to make friends. I had no idea how a mother, whose kids had all left the country, whose husband had died, could replace them all with neighbors or cousins.

Piper seemed more deflated than she had a moment ago. She eyed her hands, picking at the dead skin around her nail beds yet again. Without looking back up at me, she continued, "She's a tough lady, been through a lot. And I always thought maybe things weren't quite normal with her. There were times when she was full of energy, especially before my dad died, but then the low moments were awful. Like there were days when a dark cloud came over her and even when it had passed, we all had to spend weeks wringing out the water it left behind."

I nodded, unable to imagine taking care of my mom. If anything, it frustrated me how much my mom wanted to take care of me. Guilt washed over me as I thought about how privileged I was to get to grow up so slowly. I was glad that I had not told her the story about my most recent fight with my mom.

"Who's to blame, though? I was born in the '80s in Romania, it doesn't get much more shit than that," Piper said, as if blowing off the whole situation as part of a broader historical problem.

I didn't know anything about Romania, other than that I thought it was in Eastern Europe. But I wasn't really sure that was the point. And based on what I had learned from my mom, it sounded like Piper's mom's sadness was something beneath the surface that couldn't be explained by geopolitics. Maybe this was what she meant about understanding my situation with Shelby?

She continued, explaining that people her mom's age were expected to have lots of kids. Her mom worked for the government in a steel factory at a time when the government rewarded those contributing to population growth with an apartment block and other forms of government aid. "I'm sure you've heard about this, right?" Piper asked, without waiting for an answer, assuming it was a yes.

Piper was born in the country near her grandparents but moved to Bucharest with her parents when her brothers were little. Even with both parents assembling train parts at the steel factory, they still never felt like they had enough money. And things felt worse when Ceaușescu's regime fell in 1989. Piper was eight when Nicolae Ceaușescu and his wife were executed by firing squad.

She didn't remember the charismatic leader well but could recall elementary school classes where they learned about how he was the greatest person ever to exist. At home, her mom screamed if the kids asked questions that inferred anything different. Piper believed her mom was a supporter only to discover later that she was just afraid the neighbors, who might be supporters, would overhear and no one could afford more conflict.

When the factories began closing, her mom had to improvise. The borders were opening between countries, and her mom took what money she could and even what she couldn't and imported items from Turkey, like Jordache and Levi jeans, and Adidas and Nikes sneakers. And she resold them for a profit.

I must have looked sympathetic because Piper chuckled. "Oh, my mom would be pissed if she knew I was saying I ever had it hard."

When Piper and her siblings complained about things being bad as they got older, their mom always reminded them that she spent hours in line for bread just to feed them. Piper was less angered by the poverty, corruption, and unemployment than her brothers were, perhaps because they had considered staying in Romania after high school. Of course, they didn't end up staying; none of Piper's siblings did. So, in the end, it was just her mom, who had thankfully moved back to the countryside where she could live close to a cousin.

I tried to picture Piper's mom in the Romanian countryside, chickens everywhere. And despite how lovely old age in the country sounded, I was curious about why she never moved away.

"Life outside Romania is just unimaginable to my mom," Piper said. "She just couldn't."

I thought about the eight hours it had taken to drive to Montreal, including the border crossing. I couldn't imagine changing countries permanently.

Piper continued, "She doesn't even love hearing about life here. It all just seems like too much."

I understood being lost in one's own world. Had I ever sat down and listened to my mom's stories about her childhood without defending myself, as if her life story was somehow commentary on the choices I made in my life? If only I had been half as good a friend to Shelby as Piper was a daughter or my mom was a mother. I seemed to be caught in a game of tag, playing the part of both the rejector and the rejected. And none of it seemed to get me very far.

"Do you get to see your mom?" I asked.

"Sure, about once a year. I make it over there for a week every summer. She's never come here, and I doubt she ever will, but I go there." A smile came to her lips as she thought about these visits. "The past couple times I've gone, things have seemed a bit better. But from so far away for most of the year, it's hard to really tell."

"That's nice you go for a full week, though it makes sense since I guess it's a long trip," I surmised.

"I guess, but in the grand scheme of things, seven days really doesn't add up to much. You look at someone like me, almost forty, and you realize, there isn't forever left, ya know?" she said.

Forty didn't sound that old to me, but then I realized she was talking about her mom's life.

"I mean," she explained, "optimistically, she lives another ten years, and I get to go back every summer for a week. That's seventy days."

I had no response; the morbidity of what Piper was saying caught me off guard.

She shrugged her shoulders. "It is what it is. But it makes me think about those eighteen years I spent at home. I calculated it, and it's nearly 7,000 days. And to have seventy left makes me want to be nice."

I wanted to encourage her to go back home more often. Or suggest that her mom come spend time in Canada. Or that something change so that Piper and her mom could get more than ten weeks left together for the rest of their lives, if it all worked out as planned. But I didn't fully understand her life, and I didn't understand her mom, and I didn't know the answer.

Did my own parents think this way about their parents? Probably not, because if they did, they would certainly try to see them more often. Or maybe they did and they accepted that it was just a part of life. But how could someone grasp that? And accept it? About their own parents?

And here I was, almost eighteen, approaching the end of my days living with my parents. I pictured the wall of text Piper sent her mom, the forced embrace from thousands of miles away. I thought about the way her crow's feet crinkled around her eyes when she smiled at the thought about going home to see her mom. She was saying that she would make it worth it for that last 1 percent of the time they might have together.

## CHAPTER 11

# MOVING TO CANADA

———

"Ladiez and Gentlemen, I am 'ere today to preform za most daring, za most frightening, za most spectacular of act!" We could hear the cannon man's voice echoing through the alleyway once again. I tried to remember how many times we had heard him. My phone said it was 8:30, so only three times now. The alley was shaded but not dark, and it was hard for me to believe Piper and I had been sitting here for more than two hours. The cannon man's pitch to a new audience allowed a comfortable silence between us, and I felt relaxed despite the weight of our conversation.

Piper's eyes were focused straight ahead, and mine were on her. The smile lines etched on her face signified that it couldn't have been all bad, leaving her home and leaving her family. Instead of picking at her nails, she was completely still, maybe lost in a happy memory. I tried to imagine what she was thinking, but despite several hours together, I was certain I understood her less than when we first sat down.

It was always easier to understand or believe I understood people in my world, people who wanted what I wanted. But when the motivation shifted, when the goal became ephemeral happiness, I was lost. I gave up, my mind wandering to when I too would inevitably leave my parents.

Unlike every one of my classmates, going away to college seemed like a daunting chore to me, rather than an escape to freedom. Not that I could really imagine it, since coming to Montreal with my parents was the closest thing I could compare to leaving home. Despite this, I hoped to go to Wesleyan. With the hour commute, I would likely be able to come home on the weekends if I wanted to.

I'd made the drive many times with my parents. My mom was obsessed with an Italian restaurant in New Haven, about halfway to Wesleyan, when you take the coastal route, which we always did despite the traffic. She and my dad had met at Yale, and they had celebrated her birthday at the restaurant their first year together. Since then, every year my dad threw her a birthday party there. They became regulars with the waitstaff and owner, who knew them from before I was born.

My dad guest lectured at Yale, as well as in Boston, so I imagined meeting them for dinners when they trekked the short distance north. In fact, I had only toured colleges within driving distance from home.

Proximity to home didn't even seem like something Piper had considered when she left Romania. I turned to face her more directly but allowed her time to refocus her attention on our conversation. Finally, our eyes locked again and I asked her, "How'd you do it? Leave home just like that, I mean."

She only chuckled at the question, shaking her head. "What do you mean how'd I do it? I just did it." Her tone was matter-of-fact, as if I too were laughable.

Her siblings studied outside Romania as well, and it was only becoming more common nowadays since Romania joined the EU in 2007. It seemed like a natural decision for her, especially since she was lucky enough to get an international scholarship that still acknowledged her Romanian diploma. The fact that it was far from home was just that: a fact.

Piper was lucky she was the oldest in her family. When she left, she only experienced a portion of the guilt her siblings felt, leaving their mother at home by herself. Piper didn't say it, but I could tell she had wanted to leave. And that thought tortured her. But clearly not so much that she went back for more than a week a year.

I reminded her that I was almost the age she was when she left home. "I just feel like it's something I'm supposed to want. It's what every eighteen-year-old wants. To leave home. But I have no idea how I'll manage. So I guess I'm wondering how you did."

The smile she had shown to prove the ridiculousness of my previous question was wiped from her face. She laughed, but it wasn't a happy laugh. "Terribly," she said, so I apologized for prying.

So much of what Piper told me about her youth seemed to contradict the confident and happy woman sitting next to me.

She dismissed my apology, explaining, "It wasn't bad that it went so terribly." She spoke in a straightforward tone, but her words were riddles to me as she tried to get me to grasp what she really wanted to say. Struggles, loneliness, sadness, uncertainty, bad decisions can all be good things. I thought of Shelby and wondered if she too would someday describe her teenage years in such a way.

I was pretty good at helping people figure out their thoughts. I had plenty of practice between my half-listening to Shelby and the strangers whose minds I spun into my stories, weaving the most intimate details of strangers I observed into neat digestible chunks. I tried to understand Piper.

"What was so terrible about it?" I asked.

Piper may have felt alone when she lost her father, when she struggled to figure out who her friends were, when she pleaded for laughs from her mother, but on the whole, she had actually had an incredibly full childhood in the in-between moments. When she arrived in Canada, her mother sunk deeper into concentrating on nothing, and her siblings had become teenagers, trying to find their own ways in life.

"I was left with no friends and no family to call," she said, giving me no room to object or question or sugarcoat what she was saying. "It wasn't like I didn't try," she insisted. And she did. She even rattled off her attempts to prove it to me: She asked her classmates to lunch, she got a roommate, she joined a cultural club, she even attempted to pick up running because she noticed a group from her building often ran together, despite the cold air of a Toronto fall. But nothing stuck. At first, she introduced herself as Daria, the name she had grown up with. But as time passed, it became a game for Piper; each time she discovered a new group to befriend, she picked a new name. And with that name, came a persona she hoped one day someone would like.

"Nothing worked. No one liked me, or whatever my name was," she said with a smile, as if it were what she strived for.

I assured her that this wasn't true. I would know.

She just shrugged her shoulders. She cared so much then because she wanted so badly to have friends, but now she wasn't even sure she would have liked any of them anyway. I wondered if they would have liked her more if she had just been herself, the self I believed she was being with me.

During November of her first year of university in Canada, while walking back to her building, Piper spotted a wallet on the snow-covered sidewalk. It was a bejeweled pale pink that had been stomped on by the slush-covered boots of passersby. Piper reached down, wiped the briny wet off with her sleeve, and opened it up. Inside was some cash, a single credit card, and an ID.

I eyed her suspiciously. "Oh, I didn't take it," she said, rolling her eyes. She rolled her eyes again, with more flare this time, continuing, "Well, I did, but only so I could return it!"

Back in her room, Piper pulled out the ID again. Atop the ID was written *Ethel Gauthier*. It wasn't hard to find Ethel's phone number in the phone book. Piper dialed the number and after two rings, she heard a soft, sing-songy voice on the other end.

"Hello, hello!" Ethel sang impatiently into the phone several times, not giving Piper a chance to speak. She reminded Piper of the cartoon princess from 1960s re-runs of a show that had been the foundation of Piper's early comprehension of the English language. Piper hadn't thought of that show in years.

Ethel had given up with the "Hellos" and asked, "Is anyone there?"

Piper's mind was still on the princess show and the princess's opera singing companion, Mr. Piper. A smile crept across her face.

"Piper," she answered. "This is Piper."

"May I ask why you're calling, Piper?" Ethel asked. Her impatience disappeared immediately when Piper explained how she had found the wallet and was calling to give it back to her. Ethel invited Piper to tea to get her wallet back and to thank her. Despite noticing a birth date on Ethel's ID that made her nearly forty years older than Piper, she decided to take her up on the offer, and their connection was immediate.

For the rest of the year, Piper spent each Saturday afternoon sprawled out on the sofa in Ethel's studio apartment. With only a pink bejeweled wallet to go on, I imagined Ethel to be glamorous. Maybe she was the one who first showed Piper how to wing her eyeliner or shape her brows.

Piper had only been in Canada a few months when they met, so their afternoon tea often stretched into evenings. They navigated the underground city of Toronto together when they wanted to get out but avoid the wind and sloshy streets.

I wondered why Ethel lived on her own in a studio and what she had spent her Saturdays doing before she had met Piper. Piper didn't say, but in my mind, Ethel never married or had kids, and I felt hopeful that they had found a familial connection in one another.

Piper's eyes lit up as she spoke about their friendship, leaving out any defining traits of Ethel's appearance or broader demographics but instead talking about how their time spent together made her feel. It was the first time in her life she felt really liked. Others had thought she was funny, but Ethel thought she was hilarious. Piper never felt guilty if she droned on about something that had happened that week, not yet having mastered the art of storytelling in English. Ethel was always interested.

I wondered what Ethel thought about Piper's stand-up routines, but when I asked her if Ethel had ever seen one of her shows, Piper shook her head.

"It was just that one year in Toronto. Ethel moved away, and I actually made some friends on the third-tier comedy circuit. Remember?" Piper winked.

My mind was still on Ethel. I felt like I was beginning to understand Piper and to understand who really inspired her name, who became her interim stand-in for family, and who helped create this imperious force beside me. "Did you two stay in touch?" I asked.

"No, we didn't." I knew my face showed some regret at her response, but Piper smiled, a true, happy smile. "Not everyone is meant to be in your life forever." And Piper moved her focus from an invisible spot on the ceiling back to me.

I thought about how this story had begun; how Piper was separated from the few people she knew best; how a stranger had made a new city feel a little less lonely for her; and how a stranger inspired her to change her name to one that she came to own. I wondered if Ethel knew how badly Piper had needed her.

Or maybe, just maybe, Ethel had needed Piper too.

## CHAPTER 12

# PIPER'S CONFIDENCE

———

A roar of applause resounded from somewhere beyond the alleyway that stretched out in front of us. We could just make out flickering bursts of fire slowly getting brighter. We couldn't quite identify what exactly was coming toward us, distracted as we were by the bolts of light and smoky afterglow. From our vantage point, seated inside the vestibule between the two sets of heavy metal doors, we could now make out two women, both dressed head to toe in zebra-print leotards and leggings, gripping batons in each hand. One of the women was absentmindedly swinging her baton around. As she grabbed and shook it, a puff of fire suddenly burst out from one end. I jumped, and Piper laughed. The two women were unfazed.

"*Salut,*" the women greeted us, now only yards away.

"*Salut,*" we replied, Piper's voice overpowering mine. As the women crossed into our foyer, I folded my legs toward Piper, offering them plenty of room to get past me, not interested in having any part of my body accidentally catch on fire.

Other than their greeting, the women hardly seemed to notice us. They were engrossed in recounting stories I couldn't quite get the gist of. They extinguished their two-sided torches only once they were through the second set of doors and into the building's central hallway.

Turning around in her metal chair, Piper followed them with her gaze until the doors stopped their swinging and remained shut. She waited a moment after we heard the click of the doors, as if she needed complete silence to ask her next question. Finally she said, in almost a whisper, eyes wide, "Now there's a job you can get fired up about!"

I raised my eyebrows. Was she thinking about a new career for herself or for me, or was she just trying out a new joke on me? Nothing about swinging around fire in front of a crowd while wearing a striped leotard and heels seemed enjoyable. But that wasn't her point, so I just laughed. She continued to stare at me, seeming to want continued reassurance that it was a viable option for one of us.

Finally, I said, "Piper, you would probably need more bravery than skill in that job."

She looked at me quizzically. Or maybe she was offended that I was not appreciating the talent and years of training of the zebra ladies.

"I just mean you couldn't pay me to do something like that." I was certain of my words. I didn't want her signing me up. I had had enough of that with my parents, though baton throwing would not have been their first choice in internships to put on my resume.

I smiled, thinking about telling my parents I was joining the circus, knowing I never would, because the mere thought of being on stage to do anything, much less toss fiery sticks in the air in a skin-tight zebra suit, brought on vertigo. I never understood people's willingness to risk embarrassing themselves in front of friends or strangers.

Every fall, my high school used a small portion of its programming budget to host a school-wide talent show; the rest of the budget went to sports-related events. Students often performed covers of Taylor Swift or showed off their classical piano skills, perfected by years of private lessons. My sole incentive to attend was to support Shelby.

Shelby was an incredibly talented hula hooper; she never even took a class but had spent years practicing and watching YouTube videos. Since we were freshmen, each year her performances became more extravagant. Techno music blasted while neon hula hoops spun at lightning speed around her arms, ankles, and hips. Despite the natural maturation of most of the girls our age, Shelby continued to fit into the same black leotard her mom bought her for a dance class in middle school.

Watching her was mesmerizing; hers was one of the only performances I enjoyed. She looked happy and focused, spinning and twirling. So many of the other productions caused me excruciating secondhand embarrassment. No matter how much jealousy I could feel watching talented peers, watching them fail was so much worse.

Worst of all were the people who thought they were funny. There were always a couple kids each year who decided to try their hand at comedy. They weren't even all that bad, but I couldn't help but hold my breath for the entire performance, waiting for them to do something awkward or for them to forget what they were going to say. Luckily, the crowd usually laughed anyway, even if it was out of fear of how uncomfortable things would be if they didn't.

I knew what it was like to create something, to write a story, and to watch it fail. When I uploaded a story and almost no one liked or commented on it, or worse, if people left negative reviews, it felt like I needed to carve out a small part of myself and eject it to a place where no one would ever find it. At least I had the comfort of anonymity. The rejection was not so public.

A mental image of a young Piper popped into my head, standing up on the makeshift wooden stage in my high school gym. Black curtains draped behind her and a banner announcing the Maplewood High School 2019 Talent Show over her head. She launched into a story with more expletives than would ever be allowed on school property. In my imagination, I couldn't picture the crowd. Only Piper. I had no idea if she was good or not, and for some reason, I wasn't sure that mattered.

"How did you become brave enough to do it? To do stand-up, like, in front of people?" I asked and looked away quickly, staving off her inevitable half-joking, half-serious criticism of my question.

Instead of calling me stupid or insecure, she took a moment to think about her answer, eyes back on the little patch of green in the cracks of the alley. It was now darker, and color of any sort was barely visible. I fidgeted in my chair. My back was beginning to ache because of how long we had been sitting there in the flimsy metal chairs, or maybe I was just beginning to notice the passage of time.

Piper stirred. "Let me tell you a story."

I nodded.

"I had just begun performing at open mic nights, and I was still testing different waters to figure out what kind of comedy floated for me. Ya know? Was it crude? Childish? Self-deprecating? I tried it all, repeating jokes that stuck and experimenting with new ones each show and with each new audience. I only had five minutes per sketch, so I packed in as much as I could. I know I can make myself laugh, but I saw this as an opportunity to learn from the crowd."

Piper told some stories about sketches she had tested out before announcing that she was getting into the real story. After a few weeks of testing out sketches at a few different bars, Piper was approached by a young woman who was in one of her education classes. Apparently, someone had seen her set and talked about it at school. Piper and her classmates had been engrossed in "How to be a Together Teacher" in a Teaching Fundamentals class. She didn't know the woman very well but recognized her as someone who answered too many of the teacher's questions in Piper's opinion.

Piper thought, *Oh, boy*, as her classmate ushered her into the women's bathroom after class for a "private chat." The woman explained that she was simply "looking out for Piper" because she knew how hard it must be to move from a different country and that she could tell Piper was having a hard time making friends. Piper hadn't realized it was that obvious and could feel color rising to her cheeks. The classmate explained that maybe Piper should consider putting her stand-up performances on a back burner, because people who hang out at bars after midnight really shouldn't be her crowd.

Piper stood there listening, huddled in her hooded faux-fur-lined maroon coat in the neon-lit women's bathroom. But the moment the woman mentioned the midnight crowd, Piper had to stop her.

"Have you ever been to my open mic night?" Piper asked her classmate.

The young woman paused uncomfortably, flicked her hair over her shoulder, responding, "No, but like I said, people hanging out in bars after midnight isn't funny. You could get into trouble."

Piper knew her face was turning red but no longer out of embarrassment. She stared directly into her classmate's eyes and asked, "How do you know I'm not funny?"

There was a world outside of the usual university hangouts. Toronto was a big city. And the moment Piper realized this woman had never even seen her perform, she knew none of what she said mattered. She thanked the woman for the advice, left the bathroom, and immediately began crafting the sketch she would write about this conversation.

I tried to imagine having the confidence Piper had, even when she had been only a few years older than I was now. To stand up in front of a crowd of people and say, "*This is me*; take it or leave it." To hear someone critique her to her face and to simply move on and turn it into content.

Even when Piper moved from open mic nights, where her entire audience was either drunk or too busy rehearsing their own sketch to remember hers, to larger venues where people actually listened to what she said, she kept this confidence.

"Why would I need to worry if someone respects me, if I don't even like them?" she asked me directly.

I didn't have an answer.

"Of course, I still keep track of the crowd, you know, for feedback on what gets laughs. But there are always people out there who just want to critique no matter what. It's like they're hoping I'll fail. And honestly, I feel bad for those people because while they're so busy waiting for my demise, they are actually afraid that they are going to fail themselves." She didn't seem to notice my shoulders tense. Or maybe she did and knew this was what I needed to hear.

Was I the critic, waiting to watch others fail? Did I sit in the audience frozen by fear that others would judge me in the way that I judged them?

Piper was deep in thought. And as she turned to look at me, that thoughtfulness changed to sympathy.

"I don't want to be this way." I didn't have to explain myself. I knew she knew what I meant. From the moment I'd sat down, I'd worried if Piper liked me. I showed her how I distracted myself with the lives of others, as if that would protect me from people discovering my own inadequacies.

I was surprised when she explained that she, too, had at times worried about whether or not people judged her. She still worried sometimes.

I thought about her grouchiness when she had arrived at our post, the friction I saw between her and our guide. I wondered if she too had been intimidated, fearing this woman was judging her. Despite the confidence Piper carried, she hadn't mastered it perfectly. And somehow that was even more reassuring.

Piper understood that the way she lived her life upset people; there were colleagues who didn't like her method of teaching, there were peers who wouldn't find her comedy funny, and she would meet people who found her attitude too abrasive. Wasn't this a part of every aspect of her life?

But she also enjoyed the pleasure of a fun classroom, enjoyed the freedom of stand-up, and, who knows, might enjoy the possibility of waving around fire in a zebra suit. And by being authentically Piper, when she clicked with someone new, that conversation would be spectacular. She smiled at me when she said the last part, and I felt a surge of warmth in my chest.

Piper thought our conversation was spectacular.

## CHAPTER 13

# AND SHE WAS OKAY

———

It became overwhelming to even think through everything my conversation with Piper brought to light in my mind. I thought observing others, even listening in, would help me understand the people around me and people in general. But I spent so much time picking them apart, judging them, making decisions for them in my stories, while attempting to be as anonymous as I could so they couldn't do the same to me.

"Violet, I have to ask." Piper paused. "You seem so hesitant to just be yourself. I think I get glimpses of it sometimes, but then I lose you again. What's stopping you from just being yourself?"

Her frankness took me aback yet again. Had she been able to read my thoughts? I didn't have to think much about her question. The answer was obvious.

"I'm afraid, I guess." While I knew this to be true, the answer sounded so stupid when spoken out loud.

Piper assessed my expression and kindly didn't force me to continue. "One of the best pieces of advice I ever got was not to put myself in a box," she said. "If I sat down and decided who I was and what I was going to do with the rest of my life when I was seventeen years old, and even worse, if I stuck with it, I would be living a much less interesting life."

Without bravery, without a willingness to move across the world, put herself out there, work so hard to find friends even when the only one she seemed able to find was three times her age, climb up on a stage, and bear her soul to strangers, she would have missed the things in life that have made her feel the most content.

"And I certainly wouldn't have ended up here with you," she added, "enjoying this conversation so much." She flashed a warm, generous smile.

I looked into her eyes, which were lit up by the excitement of her own wisdom and self-satisfaction. But as she spoke, she began to notice that I didn't reflect the same energy. Hearing her talk about embracing uncertainty was only making me more aware that I was fundamentally stuck. I had worked so hard to create this box and to squeeze myself inside it. My breathing sped up, and I felt a tightening in my chest. I was so focused on my own physical reaction to what she was asking me to do that I jumped at the sound of the cannon man, ready to start one of his final performances of the night.

My chest loosened a little but then tightened again. The cannon man had taken me outside of myself enough to bring me a little relief.

Piper pretended to relax herself by shaking out her hands and saying gently, "Let's do an exercise."

I nodded at her. Exercises were fine. They were just that, exercises, not real life.

"What is your box? Where do you set the limits of your life?" Piper asked, as if she had done this before. I had anticipated a breathing exercise or some other coping mechanism my mom might have taught me. But I forced myself to be open to the question.

I thought for a moment. The easiest limit I could come to terms with was my future. When I looked around at the people in my life, every one of them knew what they wanted to do or where they wanted to go. And even if they didn't, they seemed not to mind that one day, being a lawyer, a doctor, a business person would become a fundamental part of their identity.

I enjoyed, instead, a prolonged transition into adulthood. I couldn't understand why my peers were so ready to throw away the joys of being a child, anxious to leave home and trade it all in for the burden of self-sufficiency and decision-making. When I would inevitably have to make the leap, I imagined placing a cookie cutter around my body, carving away at the edges of who I was, morphing me into who I should be.

But what was worse was that this obligatory molding didn't stop with my actions. It was at the core of who I was. I didn't know myself and was too afraid of actually figuring it out, so I put my efforts into becoming someone I could handle.

"I think I just don't want to be me. And that's hard, because I don't even know who 'me' is. So I guess the box I am in is the same box that everyone else in my town seems to be in. The box of everyone just trying to be 'normal.'" I used finger quotes as I said the word "normal."

I was finished talking, but she continued to look at me as if I needed to say more. As I opened my mouth to keep going, I felt burning in my face, and I breathed deeply and looked up in an effort to prevent tears from spilling over their waterline. For the moment, it was working.

"So you want to be ordinary?" Piper interrupted with a genuinely convincing tone that made me answer without a thought.

"I'm afraid that I'm not spectacular enough to be extraordinary," I said.

I thought about the people who got to live in vast circles, instead of boxes. People like Shelby, who was known and admired for her self-expression because she was good at it. People who were beautiful or fashionable or confident enough to earn the title of "cool" or "quirky," instead of "weird."

Piper continued to stare at me, but for fear of crying, I couldn't keep going. I re-adjusted in my seat, turning to face straight ahead. She continued to sit tilting in toward me. A single tear escaped. Piper waited for me to wipe it away.

Finally, she spoke. "I would not assume everyone in your town wants to be in a box either."

A wave of guilt clawed at my throat, screaming at me for how selfish and self-centered I had been. I had overlooked this simple, obvious realization. And it not only affected me, but it also affected every character I had ever written and every character my readers had ever read. My mind jumped to one story in particular. It was a blog post from Winter 2019 based on a quick conversation I witnessed in the school hallway, right before Shelby and I fell out of touch and I had put my blog on hold.

### AND SHE WAS OKAY

Florence's eyes glanced down at the 5'2" boy before her. She had never seen him in her life, and from the middle school pudge that was only just beginning to melt off his cheeks, she could tell he was a freshman. He smiled up at her, taking in her straight white teeth and pink eyeshadow. Or maybe he saw the pimples that lined her forehead, beginning to show through her cakey foundation.

She had just said goodbye to Mark, her boyfriend, who was headed to basketball practice, and was packing up her bag before taking her navy BMW for a spin. She would return to school to pick up Mark after practice in a few hours.

Just as she was about to excuse herself from the freshman boy, wondering if he thought she was someone else, or if he was going to ask her for information on debate team tryouts, he blurted out, "I heard you crying."

Florence stared at him.

"I heard you crying outside the science building earlier. I was just inside, but the window was open."

Florence was taken aback; she had, in fact, been crying outside the science building. She was on the phone with her mom. But she found it rather rude that anyone would listen in on her conversation.

The boy picked up on her scowl and quickly corrected himself. "I heard you crying, but I didn't hear your conversation or anything." He took a deep breath before saying, "I cry sometimes, too. And I just wanted to say, everything is going to be okay."

With that, he turned around and walked down the hallway and out of the school. Florence followed him, forgetting to close her locker, in which a maintenance person would later glimpse lining the bottom a used lip gloss, a UPenn banner, a nearly failed math quiz, and a negative pregnancy test. She walked in a daze down the hallway, and when she exited the building into the parking lot, she watched the boy climb onto a school bus, which promptly departed.

The clouds hung heavy with the promise of snow, and it wasn't until a single flake landed on her forehead that she wandered in a daze to her car.

She sat in her car for the remaining two hours of Mark's basketball practice. She sobbed in a way that Mark had never seen her. Then she sat in silence. She let snow, which had begun to fall more heavily, collect on the windshield, blurring her image from the outside world.

Florence didn't want to die. But she didn't want to live either. She navigated the world of teenage indulgences. Of Ivy League acceptances. Of a shiny BMW. She thought of the boy who told her he saw her crying. She wondered if someone else could see her now, as she locked eyes with herself in the car's rearview mirror. She watched tear droplets fall from her eyes and caught them, examining their wetness in between her fingers, like melted snowflakes.

At 5:30, she wiped the mascara that had smudged from under her eyes. She applied lip gloss she found in her center console. She picked up Mark from practice and listened to him talk about which guys should and should not be on the bench for the next game. She dropped him off at his house and drove to her home where she ate dinner with her family. No one noticed her breakdown.

She finished the school year with good grades. She never saw the freshman boy who had comforted her again, but his words stayed with her. She broke up with Mark the summer before starting at the University of Pennsylvania, where she made friends who talked about real things, who offered to study together when school was hard, and who reminded her that they too cried sometimes. And she realized she wanted to live.

And Florence was okay.

I wanted to go home and delete the story from my website. Or, at least, delete the ending. Because while in my mind Florence got a happy ending, it was only happy if she wanted to live in the confines of the box I put her in. To go to a good college, to end up with healthy relationships—it all seemed so boring. Florence's traditionalism became her personality, and I didn't give her the opportunity to want more than I had convinced myself I wanted. Fitting in had become the grand prize.

I thought back to my first story about Mrs. Goshen, the math teacher. I had assumed her life-long dream was to graduate from working at our middle school, just like me. But that was where my imagination ended. Why not leave to join a rock band? Or move to Italy? Or write poetry?

All the while, I had sought to understand people without giving them the chance to be understood. I was the unreliable narrator. I thought about my stories, each character facing their own unique battles in an attempt to get on the path to something universally acceptable. But who was I to believe they all wanted to go in the same direction?

As quickly as the guilt had come, it vanished and was replaced with a feeling that surprised me. I spent so much of my life staring at and listening to the people around me, trying so hard to figure out who they were, where their cracks were and mending them for them. And somehow through it all, I assumed that none of them was like me, each secretly wishing to break free of the box they had put themselves in. That I too had put them in. The idea that the world was filled with these dynamic people with unrevealed depth, depth I could never fully understand. What did it mean to be okay?

What about the people who didn't fit into boxes? I thought about the dismissive women with the clickers. About the man in the trailer with the rat tail. About the teenager with saggy pants who I had found creepy. About how I had judged them all instantly, even harsher than I judged people who expressed themselves on stage. I hated to admit it to myself, but I had even felt that way toward Piper.

I created fictionalized characters of people around me but then judged them in reality.

I thought about the desire Piper felt to please her parents, but then the complexity and guilt of abandoning her own mother. I thought of the loneliness she expressed upon arriving in Canada, of the insecurity she faced when she started doing stand-up, of her efforts to understand and connect with her students, of her desire to search for some sort of meaning in life, and of her desire to tell stories.

And I wanted to hug her.

I finally turned to face her directly. "You're right, Piper. I don't want to be in this box. And I don't want to force anyone else in it either."

She looked at me quizzically, and I thought about how my characters made people feel. Sure, maybe they made some people feel less alone. People online had told me as much. But my characters all got endings I had barely convinced myself I wanted. How could my stories inspire, how could my characters be relatable when they were so unrealistic? They were laughable, I now surmised.

That wouldn't happen again.

## CHAPTER 14

# QUITTING TIME

———

The night was dark, but the windows of the high-rise buildings that lined our alleyway signaled the existence of other people living out their lives separately from us. For the first time since we sat down, I took in the full scope of my surroundings. The single shadeless bulb above our heads shone a warm light that normally would have made me sleepy. I had been uncomfortably hot when I arrived, but now the summer night felt refreshing and invigorating.

Squinting at the buildings in our line of sight, I tried to catch glimpses of the people in the windows. Were we looking at apartments? What about all the spaces adjacent to where we sat? They couldn't all be auditoriums and dressing rooms. Maybe they housed other entertainment spaces or office spaces. I imagined rooms full of actors, dancers, and comics, all preparing for their shows or for the late-night gigs they were able to get—gigs that I hoped Piper would get. I hoped Piper would win the lottery and get to meet Gad Elmaleh, the comic whose name I had misunderstood before Piper had let me in on the sphere of stand-up.

From down the alleyway, a small figure jogged toward us. Even before light crossed her face and she stopped and caught her breadth, I recognized the woman who had brought Piper and me to this very spot. I pictured us from her point of view, the two of us still sitting in the silence she left us in. She had spent the evening running around the whole festival making sure people were where they were supposed to be, meeting new volunteers, and saying farewell to others as they were released from their shifts.

By my cannon-man calculations, we still had about an hour left of work. Maybe she was coming to check in on us? Or move us to a position in more immediate need of monitors. After all, many of the big performances were starting, so fewer street performers would be switching shifts and costumes.

I sat up a little straighter as she crossed the threshold. I didn't feel Piper react. Our guide let out a deep breath before a wide smile returned to her face. "Felicitations! Congratulations! You are finished."

Her hands clasped each other, her clipboard tucked under one bicep, and she rocked back and forth slightly, waiting for a response. Despite her uneven breathing, her expression felt genuine. Her olive-toned cheeks were rosy, her perfect ponytail had become disheveled, and she looked as if she was having fun.

I tried to imagine how someone whose job it was to deal with volunteers, who, like me, might not be very interested in being there, could be so joyous about the whole thing.

Piper and I were both silent. I debated combatting our guide's statement, saying we were not in fact done because what if just when we were least prepared, unauthorized personnel tried to sneak into the building? I didn't see any replacement guards, and we were actually quite good at our jobs. In reality, though, I knew my silent protestations were because I didn't want to leave Piper. Not yet.

Even if it were not the case, I liked to think Piper was thinking the same thing.

Our guide pulled the clipboard out from under her arm and took a pen from her pocket, which she used to cross something off. I imagined she was crossing off our names, signifying she had relieved us from our post. How many other names were on her list? I hoped the clicker women had overcome the awkwardness and embraced vulnerability. I didn't bother imagining what that would look like for them; any guess I might have I was now certain would not live up to their realities.

Instead of protesting or asking questions, Piper snapped out of her thoughts and blurted out, "Great."

She turned toward me, beaming in a way that could only have been seen as mischievous. I raised an eyebrow at her.

Piper turned back to face the guide, who was now smiling even wider, choosing to reflect the joy in the room, rather than the confusion.

"I actually have a question. Are there any shows we can get into?" Piper asked the guide.

The guide explained in French that there were a couple shows we could get into with our volunteer badges. I didn't completely understand what they were talking about, but I did catch the word "improv" and watched Piper's smile grow even wider. An abrupt static followed by mumbled French sounded from a walkie-talkie strapped to the guide's pants. She said a quick goodbye to us and, as she turned to walk down the alleyway, looked over her shoulder. "Your raffle ticket will be emailed to you," she called in English.

I made a mental note that if I won, somehow, some way, I would gift my ticket to Piper.

I watched her figure disappear around the corner at the end of the alley before indulging Piper in whatever plan she clearly had brewing. In her anticipation, she had inched all the way to the edge of her chair and was at risk of falling off.

"I don't know if you understood that lady, but you and I have a fun evening ahead," she said.

"You and I?" I was surprised to hear I was included in whatever she was plotting.

"Of course, I'm not going to miss out on seeing you have fun for the first time in your life," she said, winking.

Something in my stomach stirred. Nerves? Excitement? I had no idea what to expect, and diving back into the hoard of people, now shadowed in darkness, would not have typically been my idea of fun. But doing all that with Piper? Hadn't she said she could make anything fun?

"Alright. I have to go back to the apartment in about an hour, but I guess I am free until then," I said and gave Piper a smile, which I realized, after she chuckled, came out a little more sheepish than I had intended.

"Then we better get going." Piper jumped up but paused a moment to fold her chair back up and lean it against the wall where we found it. I imitated her, minus the jump, and we set out into the chiaroscuro of the festival.

## CHAPTER 15

# THROUGH A BRICK WALL

———

I followed Piper down the half-lit alleyway, the sounds from the festival reverberating at higher volumes as we neared where the alleyway led out into the street. I breathed in the smell of food trucks and smoke from fireworks we must have missed. As we arrived at the crossroad between the alley and the main street, my heart sped up. Diving into an ocean of strangers and noise frightened me, but I turned to Piper as we stepped out onto the main street, turned left, and walked purposefully into an endlessly moving, amoeba-like mass.

The crowd seemed to have thickened and moved unevenly. Some people slowed to take in the sights. Others seemed more urgently focused on a mission, perhaps determined not to miss a show. Piper grabbed hold of my hand tightly, as if she were afraid I might lose her accidentally or purposefully, and we stuck close as people pressed up against us.

Based on her excitement from talking to the guide, Piper seemed like she knew where she wanted to go. But how she would lead us there, I had no clue. I had not realized when we were seated that Piper was more than a head shorter than I was. Despite her being at eye level with most people's shoulders, she pushed through, clearing a path for me to follow behind her, my hand sweating in hers.

Normally my claustrophobia would have kicked in at this point. But instead, I allowed my eyes to wander. Piper's hand tightened, and I felt secure enough that I would not lose her to the commotion.

Bright lights reflected off the buildings and cast different groups of tourists in shades of red and green. Street performers blended into the crowd, only distinguished by their costumes. Giant blow-up Victor balloons floated above the crowd. I spotted white flashes of teeth on the floating Victors above me and couldn't help but smile up at them.

The floating Victors lit up momentarily as they passed near streetlamps or through lights shining off buildings. I felt like we were in a massive, oddly detailed kaleidoscope. The tube rotated slowly, and I, along with everything else in the scene, cycled around. We could easily have been going in circles, lights, stages, and food trucks repeating periodically. Absorbed by the magic of the place, I wasn't dazed anymore.

Sometimes there were crossroads off the main street where barriers and some signs helped to herd people along. We continued straight, and I tried to make out the performances going on. There was no way to tell if the open spaces facing the stages were usually parks or parking lots. Everyone packed in so tightly, I wasn't sure they could tell or cared what the space had been before tonight. Their eyes were glued to whatever comedian or dance group was performing in the moment; then off they'd go again.

Piper could feel me slowing down behind her, and she stopped abruptly. So caught up in our surroundings, I walked directly into her, luckily without enough force to knock her over.

I took advantage of our standstill to squint at a massive stage encircled by an even more massive crowd. The performers appeared to be dancing, but the noises coming from all directions made it difficult to distinguish what they were dancing to. Instead, I watched faint movements and imagined they were performing to the cacophony of voices, sound effects, and cheers that made up the festival soundtrack.

In front of me, Piper was checking her phone. She looked back at me and noticed my concentration, "Do you want to watch one of these performances instead? I think it's Danse Ta Vie with Gardy Fury. He's amazing." She awaited my response.

"No, that's okay. Who were you texting?" I asked.

"Adrian, he's on clicker duty. Sounds like he's gotta keep working till they close." I couldn't catch her tone with the noise of the crowd around us.

"I'm sorry to hear that," I said. I imagined Piper had wanted to spend time with him. I would have understood if she wanted to enjoy the festival with her boyfriend instead of me.

"What are you talking about? This is great! We've got a plan." She practically had to shout.

She didn't let me in on the plan but I surprised myself by saying, "That works for me. I'm happy to watch whatever."

"Let's hope we can do more than watch," she said ominously, before winking at me.

I thought maybe I misheard her, and we continued snaking our way through the hoards. This time, I was more careful to keep up with her pace.

Piper slowed down again and veered off, pulling me down a road perpendicular to the main street. It was less crowded than the streets leading to enormous outdoor performance spaces, but it still had loads of people, barriers, and volunteers scattered about.

The volunteers stood outside the barriers, guiding people on the right path. Out of the corner of my eye, I saw the rat-tail man from the trailer. He was smiling broadly, and I thought I could hear his deep chuckle as he bent over to pick up a pinwheel a child had dropped. I noticed a younger man standing by his side, maybe in his twenties, who was laughing too. They were looking in the same direction at a scene I couldn't see. I smiled, wondering if they too were coming away from this evening with memories fresh in their consciousness.

Piper's voice sounded in my direction over the crowd. "I think we're almost there." Her eyes hovered over the lit-up placards on each building, indicating a hotel or bar. Some had awnings and looked like they hosted cafes with outdoor seating during the day. We approached a section of the highrises that did not have any signs. Instead, we saw a plain, very thin brick wall with a faded blue doorway. I might never have noticed it. Nothing signified what the building was.

As we approached the doorway, I wondered if it was Piper's home. The thought felt stupid, but I couldn't think of another reasonable explanation as to why Piper was leading me into an unmarked building.

I hesitated for a moment before she opened the door, and she caught my eye. I wasn't sure how I looked. Confused? My face could have displayed fear despite that fact that I wasn't at all afraid.

"Oh, come on, you'll have fun," Piper said with a laugh before opening the door. When the door closed behind us, she dropped my hand.

As I adjusted to being indoors, I took in the space. It was a tiny empty square room with brick walls. *Where were we?*

"Ta-da!" Piper held out her arms, as if to proudly display the tiny room. There was no need; it had taken me approximately five seconds to take it in in its entirety. The bricks were a faded rust color and the only light came from two hanging lanterns in the back corners of the room.

Piper put a hand on her stomach, laughing in an exaggerated manner at my dumbfounded expression. I chuckled awkwardly, hoping I was missing some joke and that she hadn't just gone insane in the past ten minutes.

"You're too easy to mess with," she said to me, smiling. It didn't feel like she was being mean. She was genuinely having fun. Despite laughing at me, it was more like she was laughing at herself. Laughing at this grand prank she had come up with.

"So, we're now just in the brick version of where we were ten minutes ago?" I smiled. "Did I volunteer for this?"

She liked my question and laughed. "Oh, you're going to."

Before I had the chance to ask her what she meant, she pressed a finger against a brick in the middle of the back wall. I hadn't noticed it before, but it was more worn in than any of the other bricks. I thought of all the relics tourists touch, like the Charging Bull on Wall Street or John Harvard's shoe in Harvard Square. I wondered if there was some sort of luck bestowed upon believers when they touched it. I stepped forward to mimic Piper and also rub the brick.

As I leaned in for a closer look, I jolted back again. The bricks split open and revealed themselves to be two doors which opened into a dark stairwell lined by black velvet curtains on either side.

"Come on!" Piper grabbed my hand again and practically dragged me down the stairs. I could hear a faint thump as the brick doors shut behind us and we continued into the darkness.

# CHAPTER 16

# VOLUNTEERING, AGAIN

---

At the bottom of the stairs, there was another set of black curtains, but these were closed and guarded by two men in suits. Their eyes lit up when they saw Piper, and the three greeted one another with quick kisses on the cheeks. They asked her in French who the "mademoiselle" was, and Piper assured them I was with her and that she would not offer me alcohol. This seemed to be enough, and they each took one heavy curtain, pulling it aside to reveal an enormous space.

I had never been to a bar but I assumed most of them did not look like this. It was as if we had been transported back in time to the 1920s. Even in the entrance where we now stood there were three different high-top mahogany bars, all tended by men and women in white collared shirts and black vests. Some of the men had on the kind of caps I had only seen on my grandpa and in *Peaky Blinders*. They were busy concocting drinks in pewter-embossed shakers, as patrons stood at the bar, chatting, relaxing, or flirting with one another. I noticed several seating options. Different sets of sofas and chairs sharing coffee tables were occupied by groups who seemed to know each other. Women propped up on the arms of couches. Other couples were self-involved, ignoring the strangers sharing their red leather divans.

The room was so large that it was hard to believe the bar continued beyond what was first visible. But Piper kept walking, quickly greeting a few of the bartenders. I felt very aware of my leggings and sneakers and how frizzy my hair had become in the humidity. But no one said anything to me except polite acknowledgments in French. I was with Piper, and that made me cool with them.

We walked through an open doorway at the back of the bar and down a short hallway; the walls were covered in photographs from past performances. I wanted to stop and look at the photos on the walls, to inspect if they really were from the 1920s or just showed people wearing clothes reminiscent of the time period, playing dress-up just for fun. The whole place had a nostalgic feel but in a sleek way, not at all shabby. I wondered if the bar had even existed in the 1920s and was tended to over the years, or if it had been created more recently in homage to the days of prohibition.

The hallway opened up into a slightly smaller room with only one bar at the back lined with chrome-plated barstools, like I had seen in old pharmacies. The rest of the space resembled a Greek amphitheater, where the performer stood in the center and the spectators sat in a semi-circle that rose up above the stage. The space was intimate. The stands were almost completely full despite the room having no more than fifty people in it. Piper motioned for me to follow her, and we edged into a row toward the middle of the room.

On the stage, a woman dressed like a flapper sang while a coed group of musicians played instruments behind her. I thought maybe the genre was jazz but didn't have a firm grasp of music history.

Piper beamed next to me. "They're good, aren't they?" she whispered, covering her face with her cupped hand.

I nodded emphatically and leaned back, feeling grounded in my seat. The woman's voice was beautiful. She had a raspy guttural croon, so when she hit high notes, I became even more impressed. She held a microphone in her hand and walked around, more like strutted around the stage serenading each part of the small, packed room. When there were instrumental sections, she simply smiled generously out at the crowd, radiating that she too was being entertained. I knew that was a part of the show, but she really did look like she was having fun up there. Then, when their performance ended, she and her group left the stage laughing and hugging each other.

The emcee, whom we had not seen yet, stepped out on stage. He was a shorter balding man with small, round glasses that made his eyes look beady. His voice boomed as he thanked the band, riffed, and then welcomed the next performance.

The crowd erupted in applause as two men and a woman took the stage and were handed the mic by the emcee. One of the men carried a stool, which he placed in the center of the stage. Next to me, Piper was going wild, woohooing and clapping her hands enthusiastically.

I nudged her. "Do you know this group?"

"Of course! They're insanely impressive. I was worried we'd missed them," she said.

As the crowd cheered, two of the members, a woman and man, ran along the front row, high fiving the audience. I continued to clap until the din died down. Piper was one of the last to stop clapping. She sat on the edge of her seat as the trio welcomed the audience. The crowd cheered again, and the two who gave out high fives motioned for the crowd to calm while the third held the mic and thanked the crowd for being there. He introduced himself as Gerard and the other two as Hector and Zoey.

All three of them wore black t-shirts, and I could see a tattoo poking out from under Zoey's sleeve. She looked like a rockstar with short cropped black hair, shaggy bangs, and dark eye makeup. Hector looked like he could have been her brother with purposefully messy black hair and a nose ring. Despite dressing in the same uniform as the other two, Gerard looked much more clean cut. His sandy brown hair was styled in a European fashion, and he wore tortoise-rimmed glasses. They looked like an odd crew, but to see them interact made it all make sense. They fed off each other's energy as Gerard, who was clearly the lead, welcomed the crowd and thanked everyone again.

Gerard didn't explain their first act. The crowd cheered and seemed unsurprised as Gerard ran up and down the center aisle of the small theater, saying into his mic, "Alright, let's see, who to choose, just having a look around." As he walked up the aisle closest to us, Piper grabbed my arm, and shot it into the air.

"A volunteer, I love it!" shouted the performer. "Come on up. What's your name?" he asked, motioning for me to scoot out of my row and accompany him on stage.

I sat petrified. After a moment of awkward silence, Piper answered for me, shouting back, "It's Violet. Her name is Violet."

Why would Piper do this? Had she not just spent four hours with me? Getting to know me? In what world would this be something I would want to do?

Sensing my distress, she moved her grip on my arm to my hand and said, "Come on, I'll come up with you. At least they are speaking in English." She had a point, and I had no choice but to rise with her and pardon myself as I inched past the others in my row.

It was clearly not customary to invite two guests on stage, but Piper walked up so confidently that no one questioned her. She directed me to the high stool and helped me up. Even being as tall as I was, my legs dangled, hardly touching the floor. The sister and brother duo made room for Piper next to the stool, and she stood there by my side. My whole body went stiff, and it was all I could do not to fall off my perch. Piper's hand, now on my shoulder, grounded me. The crowd had continued their cheering, and Piper leaned in and whispered, "It's all okay. These guys are awesome."

I turned my head to face her, beginning to feel a burning in my eyes. She saw my panic and continued to assure me. "You don't have to do anything, just sit here. It'll be fun," she said.

Squeezing my eyes shut for a moment, I looked down and counted to three. At three, I would take a deep breath, look up, and smile at the crowd.

I was spared the moment because Gerard had returned to the center of the stage, directly in front of me, and asked the crowd to give me a round of applause. Piper lifted her hand from my shoulder only for a moment to clap.

Gerard stepped aside so the crowd could see me, and he held the mic out in front of me. "Hey, Violet, can you introduce yourself for the crowd?"

I cleared my throat and cringed at the sound echoing around the room. "Hi, I'm Violet." Unsure what else to say. "Um, I'm seventeen." Before I could continue, Gerard gasped loudly.

"Seventeen?" Gerard feigned shock. The other two cupped their hands over their mouths dramatically. "How the hell did ya get in here?" he asked with a chuckle. "Actually, don't answer that," he said, pointing his index finger at me in an avuncular gesture. I looked down, sheepishly, but appreciated that he didn't seem to mind my age. He was laughing, and the crowd was laughing with him.

"Let's ask your mother." And he looked over at Piper. "Hey, Mom. How'd you get your child into a bar?" I wondered if he actually thought she was my mom, or if it was all part of the act.

Piper was made for the stage. She matched his energy perfectly and retorted in a fake angry tone that didn't sound at all like my mom, "How old do you think I am?"

Gerard held his hands up and retreated back. "A little older than seventeen," he said with a wavering voice.

Piper laughed. "Fair guess. Maybe, I'm her sister." She moved her face closer to mine as if to point out our family resemblance where there wasn't any. Her gesture evoked more laughter.

He then turned to me and held up his hand, pretending to whisper so Piper wouldn't hear. "What are you doing with this old lady?"

I flushed and responded, "Well, she got me into a bar, didn't she?"

Gerard roared, clapping his hands together, the sound reverberating into his mic and around the room. The crowd laughed too, and my smile began to feel a little more natural.

"Okay, well, Violet, you are clearly very smart. So tell me about yourself. Where are you from?"

Each time I spoke, he turned the microphone toward me, and I leaned forward to speak into it.

"Connecticut," I said.

"Ah, you're American. I couldn't tell," he said sarcastically, gesturing to my outfit. I wished I had taken off my lanyard, which displayed an enormous photo of fifteen-year-old me, sporting braces. I could feel my face growing redder, and I looked down at my leggings and t-shirt, a look on par with stereotypical American fashion. But still, there were some cheers from audience members who must have also been from the States.

"Alright, so actually, tell me who this lady is." He gestured at Piper, morphing his face into a dramatically confused expression.

The mic was in front of my face, and I hesitated. This made the crowd laugh. They laughed harder when I, unsure of myself, answered slowly, "My friend?"

"Okay, Violet, we're going to need to know a little bit more. Normally, I'd ask your occupation, but I assume you don't have one yet."

I wasn't sure what made me say it, maybe it was my intense focus on Gerard's words or maybe it was the reassurance I felt with Piper beside me. "I'm a writer," I blurted out.

"You write," Gerard looked impressed. "What do you write?"

"Stories," I quipped.

"Okay, come on, Violet. You can do better than that. What kind of stories? Fantasy? Mystery? Romance? Drama?" He splayed out his hands when he said the word "drama," as if he were an actor from a soap opera.

For a moment, I considered the genres he offered up. But then I surprised him and myself by responding, "Stories about strangers." I kept my eyes locked with his, instead of looking out at the crowd.

"Oh, man," he said as he threw his head back. "Well, I gotta be careful what I say around you then." The crowd laughed.

"Only nice stories," I said, smiling suspiciously.

"Well, that's good. Otherwise, I'd have to call your mother!" Gerard, Piper, and I all laughed. "Does your 'friend' over here have a name?" He gestured dismissively toward Piper.

He let me answer, and then gave me a bemused expression. "Pipe her? I hardly know her!"

The crowd erupted in laughter again. I felt my cheeks flush but I laughed with him. Gerard allowed a moment for the room to quiet again before turning to Piper. "Okay, Piper, you're up. Tell me about Violet. Let's go with one word to describe her."

"Serious." Piper chuckled. "Just kidding, let's go with thoughtful," she said emphatically.

"That's a good one, alright. So Violet, our friends Hector and Zoey are going to sing a song for you. Guys, we've got a minor, let's keep it PG," he said, winking to his sidekicks.

The crowd laughed, and I cringed thinking I had ruined their adult fun. But looking out at individual faces, everyone seemed to be smiling.

"Now, Violet," Gerard said, "I hear you're awfully serious, but don't be afraid to dance along to the music if you feel so inclined."

Piper responded with a cheer, already looking ready to bust a move. Zoey and Hector started out in full force, like it was a song they had practiced.

*From the leggings to the sneakers*
*The t-shirt and the lanyard*
*I'd bet all my money*
*That can only be American standards*
*Oh oh oh, Violet*
*Oh oh oh, Violet*

They sang to the tune of a pop song I couldn't quite place but was familiar, nonetheless. I was still seated, avoiding crossing my arms across my chest and seeming too serious. Piper looked as if she were about to make her way across the stage, waving her arms like a poorly piloted airplane. The crowd's eyes were focused on her and my eyes on them. Still, I was surprised when she grabbed one of my dangling arms and pulled me to my feet.

Hector and Zoey went with it, singing now at both me and Piper, who was forcing my arms to replicate her own motions.

*She might never be an athlete*
*In shows she'll never play a part*
*I mean look at her, she's not a dancer*
*But you just know she's got a kind heart*
*Oh oh oh, Violet*
*Oh oh oh, Violet*

The duo was beaming at me, and despite their words, I could feel myself begin to sway without Piper forcibly moving me. I reclaimed my arms and instead of dramatic movements, I kept them closer to my body but moving all the same. My legs felt looser, and I bent and unbent them to the beat. The image of a giraffe, which so often popped into my mind as I imagined how I looked dancing, was replaced by Piper, whose movements I performed alongside of her but with more prudence than she displayed.

The song continued.

*I don't know how she got into this bar*
*She might have tipped the bouncer a buck*
*But as for what I think about her older friend*
*To be honest I think she and I would totally... get along!*

The pause evoked a roar from the audience, who were now singing along with the chorus.

*Oh oh oh, Violet*
*Oh oh oh, Violet*

Piper doubled over laughing, and when she managed to regain her composure, she shimmied at the audience. Her volunteer shirt was about as sexy as mine, but her presence earned plenty of cheers from the crowd. She and I were both traveling around the stage, dancing more freely now. Hector and Zoey, still gripping their microphones spun around with our motions to continue their serenade.

*Oh oh oh, Violet*
*She makes us all smile a bit*
*Everyone get a close look*
*Next time you see her, it'll be on the cover of a book*
*Oh oh oh, Violet*
*Oh oh oh, Violet*

My cheeks burned, and I hoped the dim lights masked their redness. But the blush wasn't entirely from embarrassment; I didn't remember the last time I had laughed so much. The corners of my mouth twitched from the grin that had been plastered on my face. And then I realized what I was feeling. For the first time in a long time, I was having fun.

# CHAPTER 17

# THE END, OR THE BEGINNING

---

When the song was over, Zoey gripped one of my hands and Piper gripped the other. Hector lined up on Piper's other side, and we all raised our arms together to offer a deep bow to our audience. Everyone clapped, some crowd members offering whoops and hoots. I knew they were cheering for Zoey and Hector, the real stars of the show, but as I locked eyes with Piper, I knew that wasn't what mattered.

She and I had just performed maybe the most awkward dance ever to grace a stage, but the glow and broad smiles could not be wiped from our faces. People smiled at us as we climbed off the stage and made our way up the aisle back to our seats. Some people even stuck out their hands, offering high fives. Once we were at our row, I turned to scoot past the seated audience members, but Piper grabbed my arm and tugged it whispering, "C'mon." I followed her to the back of the room and through the hallway we had come from.

As we departed, I could hear Gerard saying, "Who's next?" I turned back for only a moment to see a sea of hands shoot up, jealous of my time in the spotlight. And I knew that there were also lots of others who were making themselves super small. I felt for them.

The hallway was dimly lit, but I paused and Piper waited with me. One photo showed a woman bending backward, her beaded veil almost touching the floor behind her. If I looked more closely, maybe I could have identified a layer of elasticized clothing, but at a glance she appeared to be wearing only beads. Another black and white photo beside it was of an eight-member band, each member sporting a white hat with a dark ribbon around it. I wondered if this hall was filled with people who had taken the stage I had just stood on.

I turned back to Piper who was still in the hallway but was scoping out the main room. When she noticed I was ready to continue, she directed me to a lounge setup with an open couch. The other two sofas and armchairs were occupied by a group of friends, but they all leaned in over the common coffee table, allowing me to squeeze onto the couch without interrupting their conversation. They were chatting loudly in English about a friend who was not at the festival with them. I half listened, but mostly re-lived the past ten minutes in my head, a smile still lingering on my lips.

Piper returned from the bar with two Shirley Temples in hand. She handed one to me, and we sipped our virgin cocktails as she recounted her favorite moments from the performance. A few couples stopped by to tell us how fun the song was. But when the interruptions from strangers and Piper's chattiness waned a bit, she looked at me earnestly and asked, "How do you feel?"

"I actually feel pretty good," I said, surprised at myself again. I remembered times when I was asked to present in front of a class, a performance I could prepare entirely, and how for days after, I would cringe at my awkwardness. But now I felt relaxed, happy to be sitting there in that dark lounge sipping my sugary drink with Piper. "What about you?"

"Electric," she said. And she was. Piper radiated energy, intoxicating with joy each person who came over to us. Despite being no more than 5'2", she had an outsized presence.

"You seem like you really like being on stage." It was a statement, but I asked it like it was a question.

"I do." She paused.

I had always thought people who liked to be on stage, who sought out activities like our school talent show, were self-indulgent. And sure, in some ways, that may be the case. But instead of the self-centeredness I once saw, I began to see something different. Self-expression.

Then it hit me. Juste Pour Rire, Just for Laughs—the name of the festival. People did things just for laughs. And that was a critical, important, and possibly essential part of being human.

I thought about Shelby, performing her hula hoop dances. And how I had always been jealous that she was brave enough to go out and get the attention all of us as humans crave. But the attention, the performance, was simply a byproduct of doing what she loved.

After all, wasn't that why I wrote? To create something that touched people.

I thought about Piper up there, dancing freely around the stage, and smiled. "Is this what it's usually like?" I asked her, genuinely curious.

"Well, I'm not typically a volunteer. But then again, I don't usually get to go on stage before 1 a.m. Unless, of course, it's open mic, but then I have all of five minutes," she said.

"I bet you're really good," I said and meant it as a compliment. Piper scowled. "I'm not sure, but I really don't care. I don't do it to *be* good at it. I do it to *feel* good." I could tell she wasn't done with her train of thought, so I let her think. "If you said you loved to go on walks, I wouldn't ask you if you were good at it. I would just understand that you love it. Similarly, I would never ask you if you're good at writing, because that's not what matters. What matters is that you love it," she finished with conviction.

I nodded, noting, "There is a component with stand-up or with writing or really with any art where there's an audience. Whether they are strangers or not. And I guess, I want to be good if there's an audience."

"Sure," Piper said, "but it doesn't start with being good. It starts with being free and letting others experience the contagious feeling of liberty." She became more animated as she spoke. "Making people laugh is what makes me feel free. It's how I get through my job. Kids love to laugh. Who doesn't? If I get to the end of the day, and I've helped someone feel something, it's been a good day. Even better if I can help them have fun."

"I'm not sure that's why I write," I pondered aloud. "I mean, maybe in some ways, but not entirely."

"Fair, you don't seem as if you like to have fun." She nudged me teasingly. "So why do you write?" she asked, becoming more serious.

"I guess, to understand people," I said out loud, realizing how truly off target I was in reality. What I had been attempting was to understand people, to dissect who they were in the fraction of a moment I saw them. As if I could fully understand who they were at a level that did them justice. No, that's not what I had been doing with my writing.

I thought back to when I began posting my stories, how sharing writing with others and taking in their thoughts and words had made me feel. Studying strangers had only made me feel alone, had made me feel like I was doing to others what my mom did to me. And I hated it. But the act of sharing them became a catalyst for me to make friends. To get to know people. To learn about the world. To learn about myself. I looked at Piper, who was still attempting to make eye contact with me even when my eyes glazed out of focus. This was why I did it. Why I wrote. That, after all, was the reason back in ninth grade I had named my blog, "To Know a Stranger." I just didn't know what that meant yet.

My phone vibrated in my back pocket. *You coming back now?* flashed up from my mom. It was already just past 11 p.m. and, according to maps, the walk back to the apartment was only about ten minutes. *Just got off. I'll be back in 10 mins*, I texted back.

Piper was looking around the bar, a slight smile on her lips. "Do you have to go now?" she asked, when I looked back at her.

"Yeah, my parents expect me home in ten minutes, so I should probably head out," I said.

"Alright, I'll walk you out," Piper offered. We left our empty cups on the coffee table in front of us and rose. I found myself walking slowly, taking in the scene for the last time. It wasn't that it was a bar. I hadn't had much interest in going to bars, and it would be several years before I could in the States. It was just so new, so different from anywhere else I had been. And I didn't hate it.

I said goodbye to the bouncers, and Piper let them know she would be right back. My eyes had adjusted to being underground, but I still had to be careful climbing the stairs in the dark. Piper walked even more slowly than I did, and neither of us said a word.

I wondered what we would say. Would we stay in touch? I didn't think so. Something about the night felt very final. Piper and I were strangers, and we would continue to be strangers, but this evening we collided.

I thought about what she had said about Ethel. How they were friends when they both needed it, when it made sense, but that she didn't believe in making something last just for the sake of it. Piper would continue to live her life here in Canada. I would go home to Connecticut and then to college, and then who knows where. It was weird to think that maybe I needed this night. Maybe I needed Piper.

Somehow, through all of this, my parents had been right. I'm not sure they realized what right even looked like, and maybe if I had been paired up with the man from the trailer with the rat tail, I would have had an equally insightful conversation. But Piper felt special. Our connection felt special. And I liked to think maybe she needed this too.

We reached the top of the stairs. Piper pulled a handle that blended in with the large black doors. I could see the bricks parting on the other side of the wall in my head as I had witnessed on our way in, and I hoped the room would be deserted when we returned to street level, although I didn't know what our goodbye would look like.

As the doors opened slowly, I could hear exclamations coming from the other side. Three American women greeted us in the brick room. They had been in the room trying to find the right brick to push and were thrilled to have the mystery solved for them. They rushed past us down the stairs and into the darkness, and we immediately took their place in the brick room.

I had been wracking my brain for what to say. What an appropriate goodbye would be. "I can't wait to see your name as a headliner for a comedy show one day," I said. We were facing each other in the small room.

Her eyes lit up. "Oh, you will," Piper responded.

We were both silent. Neither of us complimented the other or offered the formal niceties of how much we enjoyed the evening or each other's company. That didn't need to be said.

Instead, all she said was, "Keep writing. Stories are a wonderful thing."

"I will." I was certain I would. "I'll even write tonight when I get home." I paused. "Maybe not tonight, but definitely tomorrow." And I knew what my next story would be.

"Awesome, that's what I like to hear," she said as we stood there for another second in silence.

I could feel my phone buzzing in my pocket again. I was sure my parents had stayed up waiting for me to come back and were probably beginning to get anxious.

I was about to turn away and could feel Piper doing the same, but before I did, I gave her a quick and awkward hug.

She hugged me back and said, "I can't wait to see your name on the cover of a book one day."

I smiled at her. "We'll see."

I hadn't acquired Piper's confidence yet, but I was willing to entertain the possibility, and as I did I thought of the cannon man and the little girl who had given confidence to her anxious brother earlier that night.

# EPILOGUE:
# FIFTEEN YEARS LATER

It was early evening, and the sun still shone brightly over Montreal, reflecting off the west-facing windows of the buildings lining the street. Piper moved her sunglasses from her eyes to the top of her head in order to see her phone screen more clearly. Her schedule for the night was packed, but she had at least another hour to kill before her first performance. She had made a habit of wandering around leisurely before a show, and she kept an eye peeled on the street where she could see the food trucks and their long disorganized lines.

A bald head stuck out feet above the rest of the crowd. He appeared to be perusing the menus of each food truck, but Piper knew exactly what Adrian would end up getting anyway. She smiled to herself and continued walking, knowing there was no way he could see her even if he was looking. Her ripped jeans, black t-shirt, and short stature made the crowd effective camouflage.

She mixed in with other onlookers, watching first a street performance, a unicycler doing loops while juggling flaming bowling pins. The usual. She eyed a sandy-haired audience member as he attempted selfies with the unicyler in the background. Piper re-adjusted so she could see his screen, noticing the photos he took showed much more of himself than the unicycler. She edged her way closer until she was directly beside this stranger. Her height was an advantage as she could stare directly at the man's screen, but he would have to look down at her to notice. She lowered her glasses to cover her eyes just in case. To Piper's glee, the man, who was in his early twenties judging by his looks, uploaded the selfie he had taken directly to his dating profile. Who does that? Piper chuckled, her mind racing, wondering if she could somehow fit this into her show that night. She continued to watch the man's screen, a much more entertaining show than the unicycler. He began scrolling through profiles of women at least double his age. She discretely took a look at his face again, which still had uneven stubble and cuts from nicking some residual acne while shaving. Her focus returned to the women nearly her age. She had to use this tonight, she thought, smiling and inspired by his youth and perhaps misplaced desire for experience.

She had seen enough. She continued down the main street toward the food trucks. As she went, volunteers stood at the entrance of various buildings, handing out flyers and pamphlets announcing upcoming shows. Piper broke from the stream of people to greet one of the volunteers on the sidewalk. She grabbed a flyer from one of the young women, smiling broadly. After a gracious thank you, Piper returned to the crowded street and stuffed the pamphlet in her jeans pocket. She knew she was ready for tonight.

She arrived at the food trucks when she ducked aside and tucked herself between the first truck and a stand selling green plush Victors. Her arms crossed and her weight resting on her back foot, she took in the environment. She had been to this festival every year for as long as she could remember, except when she missed it for her sister's wedding and her mother's funeral a few years later. The buzz of tourists, all excited about comedy, filled her with immense happiness. It was a world of people who loved what she loved.

She was so fixated on the faces of people walking by that she jumped when she felt a large figure looming directly behind her. Before she could react more befittingly, she was greeted with a kiss and a large serving of poutine being handed to her. A smile found its way to her lips, followed by a gravy-soaked French fry. She thanked Adrian with another big salty kiss.

"That line was crazy," he remarked, scratching the back of his bald head. Piper noticed a red glow on his forehead and berated him for not wearing a cap.

"Do you even have sunscreen on?" she asked, patting her pockets in vain, knowing there was no way she would have thought that far ahead. She had learned the importance of sunscreen after years of outdoor recess. Watching children fall over each other was a lot less entertaining when she could feel the nape of her neck searing, and Adrian's scalp was less protected and two feet closer to the sky. He shook his head and shrugged.

Adrian was not a Juste Pour Rire connoisseur like herself. He had attended the festival about half the times she had. She didn't mind this either, especially years back when she had just started performing. The idea of him sitting with a silent audience was a lot less appealing than the freedom to come home and tell him she crushed it, even when the audience didn't quite get her. Even now, while she was still doing late-night shows at smaller venues, she had built up enough of a name for herself that she could count on the show going well.

Just then, a dad brushed past them, holding a child's hand. Atop his head was a green shaggy hat with pointed red horns. The hat flapped over the man's ears in an incredibly impractical way for the 80-degree day, but Piper nudged Adrian and pointed at the man's head with her free hand, "We've gotta get you one of those. C'mon," she said, amused that she could solve a problem and make Adrian look like he was having fun.

She grabbed his hand and pulled him along, back up the way she had come, away from the food trucks. She knew she had seen a souvenir shop on her way but couldn't quite remember where it was. Taking breaks to scoop cheesy bites into her mouth, she spotted it. Adrian, who was less enthused by the idea of a Victor cap than she was, offered to wait outside and guard the poutine. Piper handed off the treat, not before scooping a few loaded fries into her mouth, and she popped into the shop.

Normally, the store sold Montreal-themed souvenirs but over the summer they added Juste Pour Rire paraphernalia to the mix. She sifted through the wall of Canadian flag tote bags and pillows, the "Ha Ha Ha" magnets, and the stuffed Victors. There was a clothing section in the back, so she decided to try her luck finding a hat back there. A few Canadian flag baseball caps perched on top of a shelf but that was a lot less fun than the green fluffy hat she had seen on the dad earlier.

Piper headed into the back room to grab one of the baseball caps and look around for other options. When she saw a bookshelf, she paused. The wooden unit had three shelves, all filled with Canadian comics, and guide books, and the like. But a cover caught her eye.

Two metal chairs sat vacant beside each other in a small cement space. The photo was artistic, catching evening light shining into the entrance of a building. While nothing about the photo was remarkable, she felt a jolt of déjà vu. Her eyes scanned the title and the hairs rose on her bare arms.

*To Know a Stranger.*

She lifted the book out of its shelf and checked the bottom. In small print, she read the name *Violet Bell.*

Though it had been fifteen years, Violet Bell was a name she would never forget.

She glanced through the entrance to the back room and out the front of the store window. Adrian was now accompanied by a man, who was also bald and about his age. The men were laughing, taking turns talking and eating, one poutine, the other a burrito.

Still clutching the book in her hands, Piper looked around the store for somewhere to sit down. There didn't appear to be a non-cluttered shelf or seat in the space. The room she was in remained empty, so she tucked herself into a corner between a row of Juste Pour Rire t-shirts and the wall. Piper waited a moment, eyeing the cover of the book again. Her mind flashed to all those times she had volunteered, attended, and performed here over the years. Juste Pour Rire had born witness to her growth in so many ways. Was she about to see the unwitting outcome of her interest in the people she met along the way?

### TO KNOW A STRANGER

### AUTHOR'S NOTE

Dear Stranger,

If you have found this book and you think I am talking to you, you are right.

I'm not sure I thought we'd ever meet again, though I did have an elaborate plan to track you down in the case I ever won tickets to see Gad. Sadly, I cannot say that has happened yet. I do have to admit, I've looked you up over the years and actually watched some of your sketches online. You're always hilarious.

Thank you from a stranger you were kind to. Thank you for all the lives I'm sure you have made better. You started a chain reaction in the world, whether you knew your force or not. Your kindness inspired me to show kindness, which in turn I hope has rippled out.

But it's not just your kindness that galvanized me. Your humor, your willingness to stand up in front of a crowd to express your true self, and your desire to push me to do the same is what has brought us to this moment: A moment where I write a letter to you, a book to you, and sign it with my name. You showed me that I didn't need to be at the back of the audience, anonymous, that I too deserved to be seen.

I can't say I understand you better now than I did when I was seventeen, but I guess that isn't really the point, is it?

Even though we've only met once, and may never meet again, I am so glad to know you.

To know you is enough.

## CHAPTER 1

"Excuse me!" I found myself pleading with two women in bright orange volunteer shirts. "Do you know where the volunteer van is?" I strained my ears in their direction, but noises flooded my mind. Boisterous laughs, screaming children, languages I didn't recognize, all flowing in the same direction: In.

Before Piper could read on, Adrian was beside her again, his large hand covering a mostly-empty plate of poutine.

"Did ya find anything good?" he asked, his eyes hovered over the Canadian flag baseball cap, looking hopeful.

"I did," Piper said with certainty, shutting the book and tucking it under her arm. She motioned for Adrian to follow her to the checkout counter. He offered to meet her outside the store, thankful she had forgotten her mission of finding him a fluffy hat.

Piper paid and as she walked out of the store, she felt pride. Piper looked down at the cover of her new book, knowing it would be one of her favorite stories yet.

# ACKNOWLEDGMENTS

———

Diane and David Senior
Alexander Balfanz
Elizabeth Stone
Sarah Bouchard
Jonathan Stern
Nella and David Stern
Hanna Stern
David Elias
Sophia Miller
Sara Feraca
Christine Yang
Rita Solodar
Rachel Sutor
Anabel Thurman
Marisol Thurman
Michael Tan
Emma Schmaltz
Audrey Senior

Lindsey Parker Winslett
Justin Holmes
Nirja Trivedi
Sarah Shafir
Lizzy Pott
Elizabeth Griffin
Jenna Movsowitz
Julia Wang
John Zipf
Ruth Yankiver
Tobak Zagorsky family
Zhanna Branovan
John and Marion Hichwa
Eric Koester
Jessa Bock
Kaitlyn Luo
Gaurav Uppal

Made in the USA
Coppell, TX
14 September 2021

62372502R00095